MARIAN VENERATION

The Abbot & Community of Buckfast offer you this gift
to commemorate the 1000th anniversary of the granting
of the Foundation Charter of the monastery at Buckfast
1018 AD – 2018 AD
Holy Mass celebrated by Cardinal Francis Arinze in the
Presence of the Papal Legate Cardinal Anders Arborelius
Feast of Our Lady of Buckfast, 24th May 2018

FRANCIS CARDINAL ARINZE

Marian Veneration

~

Firm Foundations

IGNATIUS PRESS   SAN FRANCISCO

Cover art:
Our Lady of Perpetual Help
16th century Greek Byzantine icon

Cover design by Riz Boncan Marsella

© 2017 by Ignatius Press, San Francisco
All rights reserved
ISBN 978-1-62164-160-5
Library of Congress Control Number 2016957596
Printed in the United States of America ⊗

Contents

Introduction

The most Blessed Virgin Mary is venerated by the followers of Jesus Christ as a normal part of their practice of the faith. Aware that she is Mother of God because her Son, Jesus Christ, is the Second Person of the Most Blessed Trinity who for love of us and for our salvation took on human nature, Christians of both East and West honor Mary in names of persons, places, associations, religious congregations, and shrines that attract pilgrims. They strive to imitate her as a model of how to follow Christ.

There is a praiseworthy desire on the part of people devoted to her to know more about their Blessed Mother. They want to go deeper in meditating on the foundations of their Marian veneration. While theologians discharge their service of reflection on the data of revelation and share that with the members of the Church, the Christians who are members of Marian associations, those who make pilgrimages to her sanctuaries, or simply those who celebrate her feasts want, each in his own way, to be reassured and encouraged with good and firm statements about the grounds for Marian veneration. This book is an effort to meet these desires.

There are those whose duty it is to help the people of God with a proper presentation of Marian doctrine. Priests, deacons, seminarians, ecumenists, catechists, and leaders of various associations in the Church appreciate a clear statement of the Catholic faith that will be of help to them in catechetical and homiletic presentations. A word on how to avoid mistakes, whether in unfounded exaggerations or in narrow-mindedness regarding devotion to the Blessed Mother, is also appreciated by them. It is hoped that this book will be found to be such an aid.

After the Second Vatican Council, which concluded its sessions in December 1965, there were some people in the Church who gave the impression that what the council encouraged and emphasized was exclusively the sacred liturgy. They were silent on such traditional expressions of Marian devotion as the Rosary, pilgrimages, May devotion, and respect for statues and sacred images. Some parishes no longer had any organized praying of the Rosary and the Litany of Loreto on Sunday evenings or in the months of May and October. Moreover, the practice of evening Mass tended to block such expressions of Marian piety or even the celebration of Eucharistic Benediction. No doubt, the Eucharistic Sacrifice is the supreme act of Christian worship. But the Second Vatican Council did not intend to rule out popular expressions of the faith. Effort will be made in this book to show how the sacred liturgy situates and encourages respect for the Blessed Virgin Mary. Christians who venerate the Mother of God will appreciate a statement on how this devotion is in line with Sacred Scripture and with the sacred liturgy. This book will give due attention to this need, since authentic Christian spirituality should be biblically based and should draw life from the public worship of the Church, which is the sacred liturgy.

There are some Protestants or Evangelicals who challenge Catholics on their Marian devotion. They suggest that Catholics give to the Virgin an attention that they consider excessive or that is not biblically based or that tends to overshadow the central place due to Jesus Christ. Well-prepared Catholics can easily see the defects in such objections or half-truths and give due answers to those who sincerely desire to listen. But there are Catholics who feel embarrassed because they do not know how to respond to such insinuations. This book strives to provide adequate answers based on Holy Scripture, the tradition of the Church, and sound Catholic doctrine. For similar reasons, Catholic ecumenists may find this book of use because it can help them to explain that Marian devotion is not a dangerous outgrowth on the organism that is Christian devotion to God.

From time to time there are reports on private revelations or on apparitions of the Blessed Virgin Mary or of the saints. Pilgrimage centers of one kind or another also arise. A Catholic needs to see clearly in such situations because, while some revelations or apparitions might be authentic, others could be the fruit of the imaginations of possibly sincere individuals. In any case, Holy Mother Church does not impose or command belief in any private revelation or apparition. The properly authenticated and approved ones can be of help. But Catholic faith is not based on them, and the Church is rather slow in approving them. This book strives to help Catholics make sure that their Marian devotion is based on firm foundations.

These, dear reader, are the reasons for the book you now have in your hands. These reflections will begin with a word on terminology. Chapters will follow on the Bible and Our Lady and on the teaching of the faith about Mary, Mother of God and Mother of the Church. Thereafter, the role of the Blessed Virgin Mary in salvation history will be considered. The sacred liturgy has a clear place for Marian devotion. Mary's faith is a great model for us. So is the example of devotion shown to her by many saints. Marian shrines and associations are other ways in which

Catholics honor the Mother of God. A chapter will be dedicated to these. Then the role of Marian devotion in evangelization and ecumenism will be considered. A brief meditation will be made on three selected Marian prayers. The closing chapter will encourage Marian devotees to go forward with joy. The hope is that by these reflections, firm foundations will have been suggested for Marian veneration.

~

I

Terminology

When we say "devotion", we generally mean the disposition of the human will to do promptly what refers to the worship of God and his service.[1] Devotion to God is at the heart of religion. It is promoted by participating in the sacred liturgy, by living according to the will of God, and by preaching.

While devotion is directed primarily to God, we can also talk of devotion to the saints, in the sense that we honor them, look up to them as our models, and make gestures to show this state of mind. In that sense, we can be devoted to the Blessed Virgin Mary and to the saints. In the popular sense, the word devotion is transferred to actions that manifest that state of mind. It is therefore acceptable that we talk of devotion to the Sacred Heart of Jesus, devotion to Our Lady of Fatima, or devotion to Saint Padre Pio of Pietrelcina.

In the title of this book, the word "veneration"

---

[1] See Thomas Aquinas, *Summa Theologica* II II, q. 82, a. 1 (hereafter cited as *STh*).

is used rather than the expressions "cult" or "worship" because in some languages and countries the word "cult" is now associated with sectarian groups, esoteric forms of worship, or even with secret societies that adopt some religious symbols. The term "worship" is better avoided because for some people it refers only to *latria*, that is, the worship given to God alone, which is the same as adoration, but not to *dulia*, the honor given to the saints,[2] or to *hyperdulia*, the honor offered to the Blessed Virgin Mary.[3]

The word "veneration" is used by the Second Vatican Council in *Lumen Gentium* and *Sacrosanctum Concilium* and also by Blessed Paul VI in *Marialis Cultus*. The *Code of Canon Law* and the *Catechism of the Catholic Church* do the same. But these documents also use the term "devotion". In this book, therefore, both terms, "veneration" and "devotion", are used to refer to the same reality of the honor given to the Mother of God.

The Old Testament did not confuse the veneration shown to some pious Jews with the adoration due to God alone. Moses, Abraham, and the prophets were reverenced. The Book of Sirach sings their praises (see Sir 44–50). The Letter to the Hebrews refers to

---

[2] See *STh* II II, q. 84, a. 1.
[3] See *STh* II II, q. 103, a. 4 ad 2; *STh* III, q. 25, a. 5.

the holy people of the Old Testament as a "cloud of witnesses" (Heb 12:1).

The theological understanding of the veneration of the saints is the Pauline doctrine of the Mystical Body of Christ, which is the Church. Because of the "communion of saints", we have a close relationship with truly venerable persons like the Blessed Virgin Mary, the Apostles, John the Baptist, the Fathers of the Church, the martyrs, the virgins, and the canonized saints. We honor God by recognizing the wonders of his grace in the saints.

Devotion to the Holy Mother of God is therefore appropriate because of Mary's role as Mother of the Savior, because she was the associate of the Redeemer in the work of salvation, and because she is our way to Christ, as will soon be considered. No doubt, as the *Catechism of the Catholic Church* says,[4] "Jesus, the only mediator, is the way of our prayer." But we should also note that "Mary, his mother and ours, is wholly transparent to him: she 'shows the way' (*hodegetria*), and is herself 'the Sign' of the way, according to the traditional iconography of East and West" (*CCC* 2674). That is why, says Blessed Paul VI, "this [Marian] devotion fits . . . into the

---

[4] *Catechism of the Catholic Church*, 2nd ed. (Vatican City: Libreria Editrice Vaticana; Washington, D.C.: United States Catholic Conference, 1997) (hereafter cited as *CCC*).

only worship that is rightly called 'Christian,' because it takes its origin and effectiveness from Christ, finds its complete expression in Christ, and leads through Christ in the Spirit to the Father. In the sphere of worship this devotion necessarily reflects God's redemptive plan, in which a special form of veneration is appropriate to the singular place which Mary occupies in that plan."[5] All this will become clearer as these reflections proceed.

~

[5] Paul VI, Apostolic Exhortation for the Right Ordering and Development of Devotion to the Blessed Virgin Mary *Marialis Cultus*, February 2, 1974, introduction (hereafter cited as *MC*).

2

Mary in Holy Scripture

Holy Scripture attributes to the Blessed Virgin Mary a place not reserved to any other woman. She is prophetically present in the first book of the Bible, *Genesis*, and in the closing book, *Revelation*. It is no coincidence that Mary is called "woman" at such key points in salvation history as the "Proto-evangelium", the wedding feast at Cana, Calvary, and in the Book of Revelation chapter 12. This point will be gradually elucidated in the course of this work.

After Adam and Eve had offended God by original sin, God said to the serpent: "I will put enmity between you and the woman, and between your seed and her seed; he shall bruise your head, and you shall bruise his heel" (Gen 3:15). God, who did not abandon mankind after the great fall, was promising a Savior who would crush the head of the serpent. God was putting enmity between the woman who would be Mother of the Savior and the serpent. Mary was already from the beginning included in the promise of the Savior.

Among the chosen people of God, down through

the centuries, the prophets kept up the hope of the people in the coming of the Messiah. In the days of Ahaz king of Judah, when this king found himself in military difficulties, God sent the prophet Isaiah to reassure him. "Ask a sign of the LORD your God; let it be deep as Sheol or high as heaven", Isaiah told him. But the unbelieving Ahaz replied: "I will not ask, and I will not put the LORD to the test." Then Isaiah pronounced the great Sign of Immanuel prophecy: "Hear then, O house of David! Is it too little for you to weary men, that you weary my God also? Therefore the Lord himself will give you a sign. Behold, a virgin shall conceive and bear a son, and shall call his name Immanuel. He shall eat curds and honey when he knows how to refuse the evil and choose the good" (Is 7:10–15). There is no doubt that this prophecy refers to Jesus Christ, the Savior, the "God with us", whose mother would be the Virgin of Nazareth. The evangelist Saint Matthew reports the appearance of the angel who told Joseph in a dream to take Mary home as his wife, because "what is conceived in her is of the Holy Spirit". Matthew adds that "all this took place to fulfil what the Lord had spoken by the prophet: 'Behold, a virgin shall conceive and bear a son, and his name shall be called Emmanuel'" (Mt 1:20–23).

In the New Testament, the first two chapters of the Gospel according to Saint Matthew and the first two chapters of that according to Saint Luke supply abundant narratives on the early years of Christ. His Blessed Mother was closely associated with him in these saving events. These two evangelists narrate the genealogy of Jesus Christ, tell about the archangel who appeared to Mary and to Joseph to bring the Good News from heaven, and then about the Visitation to Elizabeth and Zechariah, the Nativity of Jesus, the visits by the shepherds and the magi, his Presentation, the flight into Egypt, the years of private life in Nazareth, and the finding of the Child Jesus in the temple on the third day. The role of the Blessed Virgin Mary in this phase of salvation history is related in its essentials. Quiet meditation on these events is a strong foundation for genuine Marian devotion. Here, a brief reflection on the Annunciation, the Visitation, the Presentation and the finding in the temple will be sufficient in order to give more clarity to the theme.

In the *Annunciation*, the Archangel Gabriel sent from God to the city of Nazareth greeted the Virgin Mary: "Hail, full of grace, the Lord is with you!" He reassured the troubled virgin: "Do not be afraid, Mary, for you have found favor with God. And behold, you will conceive in your womb and bear a son, and you shall call his name Jesus. He will be great, and will be called the Son of the Most High." To the question of the prudent virgin regarding her virginity, the heavenly messenger replied: "The Holy Spirit will come upon you, and the power of the Most High will overshadow you; therefore the child to be born will be called holy, the Son of God." He also assured her that her kinswoman Elizabeth was already in her sixth month, because with God nothing will be impossible. The supreme moment had come. The whole world, as Saint Bernard puts it, was waiting for the consent of Mary. In faith and obedience, the Virgin of Nazareth pronounced her *fiat*: "Behold, I am the handmaid of the Lord; let it be to me according to your word." And the angel departed from her (see Lk 1:26–38). At that moment the Word was made flesh. The Second Person of the Most Blessed Trinity, remaining always God, took on human nature in her womb by the power of the Holy Spirit. This is a moment of major importance in the history of our salvation. The Incarnation of the Son of God is a powerful manifestation of the salvific will of God for the entire human race. The role of the Blessed Virgin Mary, as assigned to her by God, is made clear: she is Mother of the Son of God who has become man. Pope Saint Leo the Great testifies: "One and the same person—this must be said over and over again—is truly the Son of God and truly the son of man. He is God in virtue of the fact that *in the beginning was the Word, and the Word was with God.* He is man in virtue of the fact that *the Word was made flesh, and dwelt among us.*"[1]

The *Visitation* followed the Annunciation immediately. Mary arose and went with haste to Ain Karim in the hill country of Judah to visit Elizabeth, who was already six months with child. Elizabeth praised Mary's faith, and John the Baptist in her womb leaped for joy. Elizabeth, filled with the Holy Spirit, confessed Mary to be "the mother of my Lord". Mary had brought Jesus, who sanctified John. And in reply to the praise given her by Elizabeth, the Virgin Mary poured out her soul in her magnificent hymn, the *Magnificat.* She magnifies the Lord and rejoices in him, her Savior. God has regarded her low estate and exalted her. As Hans Urs von Balthasar puts it, "Mary shows her utterly unselfconscious awareness of this when in the Magnificat she extols the great deed that God has done to her, the deed all generations will acknowledge by calling her the blessed woman par excellence."[2] The Virgin of Nazareth praised God, who shows his mercy to every generation; who puts

---

[1] *Epist. 28 ad Flavianum,* 3–4: *PL* 54, 763–67, in *Liturgy of the Hours,* March 25, second reading of the Office of Readings.

[2] Hans Urs von Balthasar, "Mary in the Church's Doctrine and Devotion", in Hans Urs von Balthasar and Joseph Cardinal Ratzinger, *Mary: The Church at the Source,* trans. Adrian Walker (San Francisco: Ignatius Press, 1997), p. 116.

down the mighty from their seat and raises the lowly; who fills the hungry with good things and sends away empty those who are overly confident in themselves. And Mary recalled that God had shown his mercy to Abraham and to his descendants forever. This wonderful hymn of the Blessed Virgin Mary has been incorporated by the Latin Church into her Vespers in the *Liturgy of the Hours* every day. It opens to us a little window into the greatness of Mary's soul and how she was conversant with the Sacred Scripture, the Old Testament. The humble Virgin of Nazareth was aware of the wonders that God was working in her. She gave praise to God. And we praise God as we admire his wonderful work in the Blessed Virgin: "Ever since the creation of the world his invisible nature, namely, his eternal power and deity, has been clearly perceived in the things that have been made" (Rom 1:20), as Saint Paul writes to the Romans. The *Magnificat* helps us to know God better and also to reverence the Blessed Virgin. "The Magnificat shows us that Mary is one of the human beings who in an altogether special way belong to the name of God, so much so, in fact, that we cannot praise him rightly if we leave her out of account. In doing so we forget something about him that must not be forgotten."[3] Our Marian devotion is well based!

---

[3] Joseph Cardinal Ratzinger, "Hail, Full of Grace", in ibid., p. 63.

The *Presentation* of the Child Jesus in the temple in Jerusalem, according to the Mosaic law (see Ex 13:2, 12), took place forty days after his birth. Joseph and Mary, as poor people, presented two young pigeons. The righteous and devout man Simeon took the Child in his arms, praised God for having let him see the Messiah with his own eyes, and then made that prophecy which delivered a painful message to the Virgin Mother on her role in salvation history: "Behold, this child is set for the fall and rising of many in Israel, and for a sign that is spoken against (and a sword will pierce through your own soul also), that thoughts out of many hearts may be revealed" (Lk 2:34–35). When the Virgin Mary stood at the foot of the Cross and saw her dear Child die in excruciating pain, the fulfillment of this prophecy reached its height.

The *finding of the Child Jesus in the temple* took place when he was twelve years old. The young Jesus accompanied Mary and Joseph to Jerusalem. On their return journey, Mary and Joseph noticed that Jesus was not with any of their relatives or friends at the end of the first day. They went back searching for him in great sorrow, and only on the third day did they see him in the temple in Jerusalem "sitting among the teachers, listening to them and asking them questions" (Lk 2:46). Amazed, his mother asked him why he had treated them in that way. His reply was extraordinary and full of meaning: "How is it that you sought me? Did you not know that I must be in my Father's house?" (Lk 2:49). The evangelist tells us that they did not understand what he meant. Was Mary thinking that perhaps her Son was soon to leave their Nazareth home to spend his life in a public type of ministry? We do not know. But could it not be that she began to meditate again on what the Archangel Gabriel had said to her about her Son reigning over the house of Jacob forever (see Lk 1:33) or that she would be asking herself what her role as Mother of the Savior could mean?

The *wedding feast at Cana* is one of the "significant appearances"[4] that the Virgin Mary made in the public life of Jesus. The evangelist Saint John gives us a beautiful account. The Mother of Jesus was at a wedding feast at Cana in Galilee. Jesus and his disciples were also invited. At some stage the wine ran short. Mary noticed it and said to her Son: "They have no wine." "O woman, what have you to do with me? My hour has not yet come" (Jn 2:3–4).

As was hinted earlier in this chapter, the reference here to the Blessed Mother as "woman" is not accidental. The "Proto-evangelium" spoke already of "the woman" (Gen 3:15). On Calvary, Jesus refers to his dear Mother as "woman" (Jn 19:26). And the Book of Revelation speaks of "a woman clothed with the sun" (Rev 12:1).

This seemingly cold answer shows at least that Jesus was not yet ready to start working miracles. It also hints at Mary as the new woman, the new Eve, who has a special role in the working out of salvation history. And Mary, who knew her Son well and who had full faith in him, simply said to the servants: "Do whatever he tells you." What happened next is stupendous: Jesus ordered the servants to fill with water six jars that were there for the Jewish rites of purification. Each jar could hold twenty or thirty gallons. The servants obeyed. Jesus then directed them to bring them to the steward of the feast. What the latter tasted was excellent wine. Not knowing where all this came from, he asked the bridegroom why he had kept the really good wine until the end. The evangelist concludes that this miracle at Cana was the first of the signs or miracles that Jesus performed; it manifested his glory, and his disciples believed in him (see Jn 2:1–11).

This charming narrative is most instructive for us because it illustrates clearly a role of the Virgin Mary in the story of our salvation, and it should influence the way in which we live our lives of following Christ. Mary is attentive to the needs of people.

In her solicitude, she moves to meet their needs and wants. She pleads for them with her Son in a few words and obtains the first recorded miracle of Christ, who has just indicated that he would not have chosen to begin working signs at that time. Saint John Paul II reflects: "Mary places herself between her Son and mankind in the reality of their wants, needs and suffering. She puts herself 'in the middle,' that is to say she acts as a mediatrix not as an outsider, but in her position as mother. . . . Her mediation is thus in the nature of intercession: Mary 'intercedes' for mankind. And that is not all. As a mother she also wishes the messianic power of her Son to be manifested. . . . Her faith evokes his first 'sign' and helps to kindle the faith of the disciples."[5] This Cana event is an illustration of Mary's caring motherhood at the beginning of Christ's messianic ministry. Saint Alphonsus de Liguori quotes Novarinus as saying that "if Mary, unasked, is thus prompt to succor the needy, how much more so will she be to succor those who invoke her and ask for her help."[6] Noticeable also is the effectiveness of Mary's me-

---

[5] Pope John Paul II, Encyclical Letter on the Blessed Virgin Mary in the Life of the Pilgrim Church *Redemptoris Mater*, March 25, 1987, no. 21 (hereafter cited as *RM*).

[6] Novarinus: *Umbra Virg. exc.* 72, quoted in Alphonsus de Liguori: *The Glories of Mary*, ed. Eugene Grimm (Brooklyn: Redemptorist Fathers, 1931), pp. 135–36.

diation: the miraculous wine was of excellent quality and was superabundant. This can be read to indicate that the graces of redemption coming to us from Christ through the intercession of his Blessed Mother are indeed abundant. This Cana event is a strong confirmation of the firm biblical foundation of our Marian devotion.

The willingness to hear the word of God and keep it is one of the virtues exemplified by the Blessed Virgin Mary. Two Gospel narratives lead us to this conclusion. Saint Luke tells us that once when Jesus was preaching, his Mother and relatives came to him but could not reach him because of the crowd. "And he was told, 'Your mother and your brethren are standing outside, desiring to see you.' But he said to them, 'My mother and my brethren are those who hear the word of God and do it'" (Lk 8:19–21; see also Mt 12:49; Mk 3:34).

On another occasion when Jesus was preaching, "a woman in the crowd raised her voice and said to him, 'Blessed is the womb that bore you, and the breasts that you sucked!' But he said, 'Blessed rather are those who hear the word of God and keep it!'" (Lk 11:27–28).

It is only in appearance that these two replies of Jesus can seem to suggest a distance between our Savior and his Mother according to the flesh. For Mary is the first of those who hear the word of God and do it. Therefore, we can say that the blessing uttered by Jesus in response to the woman in the crowd refers primarily to Mary. "Without any doubt," says Saint John Paul II, "Mary is worthy of blessing by the very fact that she became the mother of Jesus according to the flesh ('Blessed is the womb that bore you, and the breasts that you sucked'), but also and especially because already at the Annunciation she accepted the word of God, because she believed it, *because she was obedient to God*, and because she 'kept' the word and 'pondered it in her heart' (cf. Lk 1:38, 45; 2:19, 51) and by means of her whole life accomplished it" (*RM* 20; emphasis added).

Mary standing at the foot of the Cross is the next biblical mention of the Blessed Virgin that has now to be reflected upon. Suffering intensely on the Cross a short time before he died, "when Jesus saw his mother and the disciple whom he loved standing near, he said to his mother, 'Woman, behold, your son!' Then he said to the disciple, 'Behold, your mother!' And from that hour the disciple took her to his own home" (Jn 19:26–27).

Every word said by Jesus is of great significance. But special importance has to be given to these words coming from him just before he died on the Cross.

"If Mary's motherhood of the human race had already been outlined, now it is clearly stated and established", says Saint John Paul II (*RM* 23). The disciple John standing at the foot of the Cross is not alone. He represents all mankind, especially those who believe in Christ. The words of Jesus are addressed not only to John but also to every one of Christ's disciples, every Christian. "Mary's motherhood, which becomes man's inheritance, is a gift: a gift which Christ himself makes personally to every individual. . . . Entrusting himself to Mary in a filial manner, the Christian, like the Apostle John, 'welcomes' the Mother of Christ 'into his own home' and brings her into everything that makes up his inner life, that is to say into his human and Christian 'I' " (*RM* 45). All this is very comforting to anyone who is devoted to the Blessed Virgin Mary.

Mary was with the early Church. After the Ascension of Christ into heaven, the *Acts of the Apostles* tells us that the Apostles "with one accord devoted themselves to prayer, together with the women and Mary the mother of Jesus, and with his brethren" (Acts 1:14). She was with them when the Holy Spirit descended on them on Pentecost day and the Church was manifested to the world. Mary is the Mother of the Church, as will be shown in the next chapter.

The woman in chapter 12 of the Book of Revelation: "A great sign appeared in heaven, a woman clothed with the sun, with the moon under her feet, and on her head a crown of twelve stars" (Rev 12:1). Making allowance for the prophetic genre of this last book of the Bible, we see the devil pitted in a deadly battle against Mary and her children, or against the Church and her members, since the Virgin Mary is the prototype of the faith community that is the Church. At the end, the dragon is vanquished.

The above narratives of Scripture references to the Blessed Virgin Mary are of crucial importance in our consideration of the foundation of Marian veneration. Focus will now be given to Mary as Mother of God and then as Mother of the Church in order to see more clearly her role in the history of our salvation.

~

3

Mary, Mother of God

The foundation of the Virgin Mary's privileges, as
well as the major proof of her greatness is that she
is the Mother of God. The rest of the superlatives
that can be said about her have their main basis in
this major truth of the faith. So has the veneration
or devotion due to her. The heresy of Nestorius was offensive to true faith
because it regarded Christ as a human person merely
joined to the Divine Person of God's Son. Saint Cyril
of Alexandria strenuously opposed this heresy. The
Council of Ephesus, the third ecumenical council
of the Church, in the year 431 confessed "that the
Word, hypostatically uniting to himself the flesh animated by a rational soul, became man".[1] Christ's humanity has no other subject than the Divine Person
of the Son of God, who assumed it and made it his

[1] In Heinrich Denzinger, *Compendium of Creeds, Definitions,
and Declarations on Matters of Faith and Morals*, ed. Peter Hünermann; English edition ed. Robert Fastiggi and Anne Englund
Nash, 43rd ed. (San Francisco: Ignatius Press, 2012), no. 250,
p. 904 (hereafter cited as DH).

own, from his conception. That is why the Council of Ephesus proclaimed that "Mary truly became the Mother of God by the human conception of the Son of God in her womb: 'Mother of God, not that the nature of the Word or his divinity received the beginning of its existence from the holy Virgin, but that, since the holy body, animated by a rational soul, which the Word of God united to himself according to the hypostasis, was born from her, the Word is said to be born according to the flesh'" (*CCC* 466, quoting DS 251).

With such an important statement of doctrine, it is no surprise that some inexact formulae later reared their heads and made further clarification necessary. The Monophysites affirmed that the human nature ceased to exist as such in Christ when the Divine Person of God's Son assumed it. Faced with this heresy, the Fourth Ecumenical council at Chalcedon in the year 451 proclaimed:

> Following . . . the holy Fathers, we unanimously teach to confess one and the same Son, our Lord Jesus Christ: the same perfect in divinity and perfect in humanity, the same truly God and truly man composed of rational soul and body, the same one in being with the Father as to the divinity and one in being with us as to the humanity, like unto us in all things but sin [cf. Heb 4:15]. The same was begotten from the Father before the ages as to the divinity and in the latter days for us and our salva-

tion was born as to his humanity from Mary the
Virgin Mother of God. (DH 301)

This definition by the Council of Chalcedon made
very clear that Mary is the Mother of God. That
great council further declared: "We confess that one
and the same Lord Jesus Christ, the only begotten
Son, must be acknowledged in two natures, without
confusion or change, without division or separation.
The distinction between the natures was never abol-
ished by their union but rather the character proper
to each of the two natures was preserved as they came
together in one Person [*prosopon*] and one hypostasis" (DH 302).

The errors were not yet over. Even after the Council of Chalcedon, there were some people who made
of Christ's human nature a kind of personal subject. To correct this error, the fifth ecumenical council, the Second Council of Constantinople in 553,
defined that there is "only one hypostasis [or per-
son] who is our Lord Jesus Christ, one of the Holy
Trinity" (DH 424). This means that everything in
Christ's human nature is to be attributed to this Divine Person as its proper subject, not only his miracles but also his sufferings and even his death: "He
who was crucified in the flesh, our Lord Jesus Christ,
is true God, Lord of glory, and *one of the Holy Trinity*" (*CCC* 468, quoting DS 432).

The true faith therefore confesses that Jesus is

inseparably true God and true man. He is always Son of God, God from God, Light from Light, true God from true God, one in substance with the Father and the Holy Spirit. He became man in the fullness of time when the archangel brought Mary the Good News and she replied: "Behold, I am the handmaid of the Lord; let it be to me according to your word" (Lk 1:38). It is the same person, the Second Person of the Most Blessed Trinity, who is God and man. "He remains what he was and becomes what he was not", sings the Roman liturgy.[2] And the Virgin Mary is the Mother of this Person born in Bethlehem. Mary is Mother of God.

The liturgy of Saint John Chrysostom proclaims and sings: "O only-begotten Son and Word of God, immortal being, you who deigned for our salvation to become incarnate of the holy Mother of God and ever-virgin Mary, you who without change became man and were crucified, O Christ our God, you who by your death have crushed death, you who are one of the Holy Trinity, glorified with the Father and the Holy Spirit, save us!"[3]

The Virgin Mary had already been acclaimed by Elizabeth, at the prompting of the Holy Spirit and

[2] *Liturgy of the Hours*, January 1, Morning Prayer, Antiphon for the Canticle of Zechariah.

[3] Liturgy of Saint John Chrysostom, Troparion '*Ho mono-genés*'.

even before the birth of her Son, as "the mother
of my Lord" (Lk 1:43). In fact, the One whom
Mary conceived as man by the Holy Spirit, who
truly became her Son according to the flesh, was
none other than the Father's eternal Son, the Second Person of the Blessed Trinity. That is why "the
Church confesses that Mary is truly 'Mother of God'
(*Theotokos*)" (*CCC* 495).

The Second Vatican Council declares that Mary
"is acknowledged and honored as being truly the
Mother of God and Mother of the Redeemer. Redeemed by reason of the merits of her Son and united
to Him by a close and indissoluble tie, she is endowed
with the high office and dignity of being the Mother
of the Son of God, by which account she is also the
beloved daughter of the Father and the temple of the
Holy Spirit. Because of this gift of sublime grace
she far surpasses all creatures, both in heaven and on
earth" (*LG* 53).

We are not therefore surprised if Divine Providence, in view of the role of the Blessed Virgin Mary
as Mother of God and Mother of the Redeemer, preserved her from the stain of original sin and from all
personal sin and made her full of grace (see *RM* 10).
Her title, Mother of God, *Theotokos* (God-bearer),
proclaimed at the Council of Ephesus in 431, has
been revered in the Churches of East and West and
in the homes of the followers of Christ. Individual

Catholic families may not all have read scholarly Marian theological volumes, but they will invariably have a holy picture or statue of the Madonna and Child in their homes.

~

4

Mary, Mother of the Church

Jesus Christ is our one Mediator between God and mankind. "For there is one God, and there is one mediator between God and men, the man Christ Jesus, who gave himself as a ransom for all" (1 Tim 2:5–6), as Saint Paul wrote to his disciple Timothy. All graces that come to us for our salvation are the graces of Christ, the one and only Savior.

This unique role of Christ as Savior and Mediator does not rule out some form of mediation subordinate to that of Christ. The Second Vatican Council says that "as the one goodness of God is really communicated in different ways to His creatures, so also the unique mediation of the Redeemer does not exclude but rather gives rise to manifold cooperation which is but a sharing in this one source" (*LG* 62). Eminent among creatures who can mediate is the Blessed Virgin Mary. This was clear in the Gospel narrative of the miracle at the wedding feast of Cana. There it was the Blessed Virgin Mary who interceded with her Son, and then he worked the requested miracle. Mary mediated with her Son in favor of the people in need.

The Second Vatican Council therefore declares that "the maternal duty of Mary toward men in no wise obscures or diminishes this unique mediation of Christ, but rather shows His power. For all the salvific influence of the Blessed Virgin on men originates, not from some inner necessity, but from the divine pleasure. It flows forth from the superabundance of the merits of Christ, rests on His mediation, depends entirely on it and draws all its power from it. In no way does it impede, but rather does it foster the immediate union of the faithful with Christ" (*LG* 60).

Mary is Mother of the Church because she is Mother of the Redeemer and his associate of unique nobility in the work of salvation and especially because "she cooperated by her obedience, faith, hope and burning charity in the work of the Savior in giving back supernatural life to souls. Wherefore she is our mother in the order of grace" (*LG* 61).

On Calvary, Jesus entrusted John to Mary as her son and Mary to John as his mother. "And from that hour the disciple took her to his own home" (Jn 19:27). John stood there for all the brothers and sisters of Christ. "Mary", says Saint John Paul II, "is present in the Church as the Mother of Christ, and at the same time as that Mother whom Christ, in the mystery of the Redemption, gave to humanity in the person of the Apostle John" (*RM* 47).

The Vatican Council goes farther, saying that this maternity of Mary toward the Church will last without interruption until the end of the world because, "taken up to heaven, she did not lay aside this salvific duty, but by her constant intercession continued to bring us the gifts of eternal salvation. . . . Therefore, the Blessed Virgin is invoked by the Church under the titles of Advocate, Auxiliatrix, Adjutrix, and Mediatrix. This, however, is to be so understood that it neither takes away from nor adds anything to the dignity and efficaciousness of Christ the one Mediator" (*LG* 62).

The Church is blessed to have so great a mother who is so close to Jesus the Mediator. The recourse that Christians have to her in trusting devotion is firmly founded on the Bible and the teaching of the faith. As Saint John Paul II powerfully puts it, "thanks to this special bond linking the Mother of Christ with the Church, there is further *clarified the mystery of that 'woman'* who, from the first chapters of the Book of Genesis until the Book of Revelation, accompanies the revelation of God's salvific plan for humanity. For Mary, present in the Church as the Mother of the Redeemer, takes part, as a mother, in that 'monumental struggle against the powers of darkness' which continues throughout human history."[1]

During the Second Vatican Council, on November 21, 1964, Blessed Paul VI declared the Blessed Virgin Mary *Mother of the Church*, "that is, Mother of the entire Christian people, both faithful and pastors" (see *RM* 47). Later, in 1968, in the Profession of Faith known as the "Credo of the People of God", he came out more forcefully: "We believe that the Blessed Mother of God, the new Eve, Mother of the Church, continues in heaven her maternal role with regard to Christ's members, cooperating with the birth and growth of divine life in the souls of the redeemed."[2]

Mary is *Prototype of the Church*. Mary is not a mere foreshadowing of the Church, as types in the Old Testament foreshadow truth in the New Covenant. Mary is in an eminent way a type, a symbol of the Church. Blessed Abbot Isaac of Stella puts it beautifully:

Mary and the Church are one mother, yet more than one mother; one virgin, yet more than one virgin.

---

[1] *RM* 47, quoting from the Second Vatican Council, Pastoral Constitution on the Church in the Modern World *Gaudium et Spes*, December 7, 1965, no. 37.

[2] *Solemn Profession of Faith*, June 30, 1968, no. 15.

Both are mothers, both are virgins. Each conceives of the same Spirit, without concupiscence. Each gives birth to a child of God the Father, without sin. Without any sin, Mary gave birth to Christ the head for the sake of his body. By the forgiveness of every sin, the Church gave birth to the body, for the sake of its head. Each is Christ's mother, but neither gives birth to the whole Christ without the cooperation of the other.

In the inspired Scriptures, what is said in a universal sense of the virgin mother, the Church, is understood in an individual sense of the Virgin Mary, and what is said in a particular sense of the virgin mother Mary is rightly understood in a general sense of the virgin mother, the Church.[3]

Mary is mother and virgin. The Church is mother and virgin.

The Church indeed, contemplating her hidden sanctity, imitating her charity and faithfully fulfilling the Father's will, by receiving the word of God in faith becomes herself a mother. By her preaching she brings forth to a new and immortal life the sons who are born to her in baptism, conceived of the Holy Spirit and born of God. She herself is a virgin, who keeps the faith given to her by her Spouse whole and entire. Imitating the mother of her Lord, and by the power of the Holy Spirit, she

[3] Isaac of Stella, *Sermo* 51, *PL* 194, 1863; also in *Liturgy of the Hours*, Saturday, second week of Advent, second reading of the Office of Readings.

keeps with virginal purity an entire faith, a firm hope and a sincere charity. (*LG* 64)

Saint Paul, writing to the Galatians, was aware of the motherhood of the Church. He calls them "my little children, with whom I am again in travail until Christ be formed in you!" (Gal 4:19). This awareness enables the Church to see the mystery of her life and mission modeled upon the example of the Blessed Mother of God. "It can be said that from Mary the Church also learns her own motherhood: she recognizes the maternal dimension of her vocation, which is essentially bound to her sacramental nature" (*RM* 43).

The Church as virgin not only is the bride of Christ, as is manifested in Saint Paul's letters and in the Book of Revelation (see Eph 5:21–33; 2 Cor 11:2; Rev 21:9), but also extols total self-giving to God in celibacy "for the sake of the kingdom of heaven", in virginity consecrated to God (see Mt 19:11–12).

Mary is our Mother. She cooperated with our Redeemer in the work of our salvation. She was given us as mother by Christ hanging on the Cross. Every baptized person is incorporated in Christ and the Church as member. Mary is the Mother of Christ and Mother of the Church and, therefore, Mother of every follower of Christ. If Abraham is "our father in faith",[4] then much more is Mary our spiritual mother in faith and charity and discipleship of Christ. All generations call her blessed (see Lk 1:48). "The Catholic Church, taught by the Holy Spirit, honors her with filial affection and piety as a most beloved mother" (*LG* 53). In the Preface of the Votive Mass of Our Lady, Mother of the Church, the Church sings: "Standing beside the Cross, she received the testament of divine love and took to herself as sons and daughters all those who by the Death of Christ are born to heavenly life. . . . Raised to the glory of heaven, she accompanies your pilgrim Church with a mother's love and watches in kindness over the Church's homeward steps, until the Lord's Day shall come in glorious splendor."[5]

The Church learns from Mary, her model. From Mary the Church learns how to be the attentive virgin, how to meditate on the mysteries of Christ, how to pray, how to be mother to those whom Christ has redeemed, and how to present her offerings to God (see *MC* 17–20). From the *Magnificat* of Mary, for example, the Church learns to apply this great prayer to herself, how God uplifts the poor, how to show preferential option for the poor, and how to refer all

---

[4] Cf. *Roman Missal*, Roman Canon; Gen 12:3; Rom 4:16.
[5] *Roman Missal*, Preface, Votive Mass of Our Lady, Mother of the Church.

her greatness to God. "As the Apostles awaited the Spirit you had promised", the Church sings in the Preface just quoted, "she joined her supplication to the prayers of the disciples and so became the pattern of the Church at prayer."

The more the Church looks on Mary, the better the Church understands herself and her mission. "Mary is totally dependent on her Son and completely directed towards him by the impulse of her faith; and, at his side, she is the most perfect image of freedom and of the liberation of humanity and of the universe. It is to her as Mother and Model that the Church must look in order to understand in its completeness the meaning of her own mission."[6]

The Church not only learns from Mary but recommends herself to her and prays to her for intercession and protection. The Church offers the Eucharistic Sacrifice "in communion with those whose memory we venerate, especially the glorious ever-Virgin Mary, Mother of our God and Lord, Jesus Christ".[7] In every Eucharistic Prayer, the Church associates the Blessed Virgin with her action and offering.

The Church as we find her concretely is nowhere totally equal to her tasks, not even in the representatives of the ministerial office. For this reason, the

[6] Congregation for the Doctrine of the Faith, *Instruction on Christian Freedom and Liberation*, no. 97.

[7] *Roman Missal*, Eucharistic Prayer I.

Church is forced to look for help, above all to her Lord, but also to her own archetypal response to the Lord, to the one who alone was able to say an unconditional Yes. Mary remains a person whom we can pinpoint precisely in history, a person who was a member of the Church, who can therefore join all the members of the Church in responding to grace, and who can train them all to say Yes in the right way.[8]

Christians learn from Mary. Mary is not only an example for the whole Church but also "a teacher of the spiritual life for individual Christians" (*MC* 21). From her, every follower of Christ learns how to say Yes to God's will, according to each person's vocation and mission. From her the lay faithful learn how to be witnesses of Christ in the family, in the place of work and recreation, in poverty as in the facing of daily challenges in life. "Women, by looking to Mary," says Saint John Paul II, "find in her the secret of living their femininity with dignity and of achieving their own true advancement" (*RM* 46).

From Mary, priests learn how to carry out the duties of their ministerial service in Church and society. They learn from her how to live for Christ and

[8] Hans Urs von Balthasar, "Mary in the Church's Doctrine and Devotion", in Hans Urs von Balthasar and Joseph Cardinal Ratzinger, *Mary: The Church at the Source*, trans. Adrian Walker (San Francisco: Ignatius Press, 1997), pp. 113–14.

how to spend their entire lives in bringing Christ to the people. Their effort to live lives of faith, hope, charity, self-denial, chastity, and obedience will gain from a robust Marian devotion.

Consecrated people can see in the Blessed Virgin Mary a model of total dedication to God. Mary will not fail to help them to be generous, persevering, and joyful in their living their vows as a radical following of Christ.

Mary is Queen. She has traditionally been honored by the Church as such because she is Mother of God, she is full of grace, she is the masterpiece of all that God has created, she is "our tainted nature's solitary boast", as the poet Wordsworth calls her.[9]

In the Old Testament, the queen mother was greatly honored. Mary is Mother of the Messiah in the New Testament. Earlier in this work, we have meditated upon chapters 1 and 2 of Matthew, chapters 1 and 2 of Luke, chapter 19 of John, and chapter 12 of Revelation. They show us Mary at the side of her Son, who is Redeemer and King. The kingdom of Christ, however, is different from the kingdoms of this world. Christ's kingdom is one of justice, love, service, humility, obedience even unto death, and victory over evil, sin, and death.

[9] See William Wordsworth: "The Virgin", in *Ecclesiastical Sonnets*, part 2 (1822).

In honoring Mary as Queen, Christians strive to imitate her virtues and to do as she told the servants at the wedding feast of Cana: "Do whatever he tells you" (Jn 2:5). Christians rejoice that Pope Pius XII, in concluding the Marian Year, instituted the Feast of the Queenship of Mary, which is now celebrated a week after the Assumption on August 22.

The Church rejoices in having the Immaculate Virgin as Mother and honors her in whom the Almighty has done great things. All members of the Church want to join all generations in calling Mary blessed and in venerating her as Mother and Queen.

5

The Role of the Blessed Virgin
Mary in Salvation History

Holy Scripture tells us about the role of the Blessed Virgin Mary in God's plan for our salvation from the first book, Genesis, to the last book, Revelation.

Genesis, in the "Proto-evangelium" (that is, in Gen 3:15), narrates God's promise that the seed of the woman will crush the head of the serpent. The prophet Isaiah tells about the virgin who will conceive and bring forth Immanuel. The Gospels narrate the great events of the Annunciation by the Archangel Gabriel, the Visitation, the Nativity, the adoration by the shepherds and the magi, the flight into Egypt, the private life in Nazareth, the finding of the Child Jesus in the temple, the public life of Jesus where Mary made "significant appearances" (LG 58), the miracle at the wedding feast of Cana, Mary at the foot of the Cross, and the Most Holy Virgin praying with the early Church from Ascension to Pentecost. And the final book of the Bible, Revelation, tells us about "a woman clothed with the sun" (Rev 12:1).

All these scriptural passages present the Blessed Virgin Mary at the side of Christ the Redeemer. "Embracing God's salvific will with a full heart and impeded by no sin, she devoted herself totally as a handmaid of the Lord to the person and work of her Son, under Him and with Him, by the grace of almighty God, serving the mystery of redemption. Rightly therefore the holy Fathers see her as used by God not merely in a passive way, but as freely cooperating in the work of human salvation through faith and obedience" (*LG* 56).

Mary is called the new Eve. Saint Paul contrasts Christ with Adam and calls Christ the new Adam: "For as in Adam all die, so also in Christ shall all be made alive" (1 Cor 15:22; see also 1 Cor 15:45). Saint Justin Martyr, Saint Irenaeus of Lyon, and Tertullian of Carthage compare and contrast Eve and Mary. Mary is the new Eve. Saint Irenaeus says that Mary "being obedient, became the cause of salvation for herself and for the whole human race. . . . The knot of Eve's disobedience was untied by Mary's obedience. What the virgin Eve bound through her unbelief, Mary loosened by her faith."[1] The Fathers of the Church call Mary the Mother of the living. Saint Jerome

[1] Saint Irenaeus, *Adversus Haereses* III, 22, 4; *PG* 7:959A–960A.

asserts: "death through Eve, life through Mary".[2] Blessed John Henry Newman says in his *Letter to Pusey* that the doctrine of Mary as the "New Eve" was a logical patristic inference from Pauline literature.

True Marian devotion is Christocentric. Jesus Christ is our Savior, the one and only Savior. He is our way to the Father. "There is salvation in no one else, for there is no other name under heaven given among men by which we must be saved" (Acts 4:12).

Devotion to the saints and to the Blessed Virgin Mary, if it is to be true devotion, should lead us to Christ and, through him, to the Eternal Father in the unity of the Holy Spirit. And devotion to the Blessed Virgin does just that. For Mary is the means, the door, through which Jesus came to us. And she is the secure way for us to reach Jesus and come into contact with the graces of salvation. Her word to us is as she already said it to the servants at the Cana wedding feast: "Do whatever he tells you" (Jn 2:5). Mary refers all to God. When Elizabeth praises her, she praises God who has done great things for her. "The veneration of Mary is the surest and shortest way to get close to Christ in a concrete way", says von Balthasar. "In meditating on her life in all its

---

[2] Saint Jerome, *Epist.* 22, 21; *PL* 22:408.

phases we learn what it means to live for and with Christ."[3]

Saint Louis-Marie Grignion de Montfort in his classic on *True Devotion to Mary*, writes pointedly:

> If, then, we establish solid devotion to our Blessed Lady, it is only to establish more perfectly devotion to Jesus Christ, and to provide an easy and secure means for finding Jesus Christ. If devotion to Our Lady removed us from Jesus Christ, we should have to reject it as an illusion of the devil; but far from this being the case, devotion to Our Lady is, on the contrary, necessary for us—as I have already shown, and will show still further hereafter—as a means of finding Jesus Christ perfectly, of loving him tenderly, of serving him faithfully.[4]

It is noticeable that of the fifteen mysteries of the Holy Rosary of Our Lady, thirteen of them, from the Annunciation to Pentecost, refer to Christ. Only the last two mysteries, the Assumption and the Crowning of Mary in heaven, are explicitly about the Virgin Mary, although she is involved in several other mysteries, especially the Joyful ones. And all of the Luminous Mysteries refer to Christ. This is no sur-

[3] Hans Urs von Balthasar, "Mary in the Church's Doctrine and Devotion", in Hans Urs von Balthasar and Joseph Cardinal Ratzinger, *Mary: The Church at the Source*, trans. Adrian Walker (San Francisco: Ignatius Press, 1997), p. 117.

[4] Saint Louis-Marie Grignion de Montfort, *True Devotion to Mary* (Rockford, Ill.: TAN, 1985) no. 62.

prise because, as the Second Vatican Council notes: "Mary, who since her entry into salvation history unites in herself and re-echoes the greatest teachings of the faith as she is proclaimed and venerated, calls the faithful to her Son and His sacrifice and to the love of the Father" (*LG* 65).

It is also remarkable that in a big Marian sanctuary like Lourdes, the central person most honored is Christ in the Eucharistic celebration, which goes on most of the day, in Eucharistic procession and Benediction, in the devotion of the Way of the Cross, and in the administration and reception of the Sacrament of Penance. Marian devotion is Christocentric. All this helps us to see that Marian devotion is normal in our living of our faith. "No approved spirituality in the Church can afford to seek God while bypassing this model of Christian perfection; none can afford not to be Marian as well."[5] It is normal that "the Church, in her apostolic work also, justly looks to her, who, conceived by the Holy Spirit, brought forth Christ, who was born of the Virgin, that through the Church He may be born and may increase in the hearts of the faithful also" (*LG* 65).

Mary is Mediatrix. There is no doubt that there is only one mediator between God and men, Jesus Christ. As already quoted above, Saint Paul made clear to

[5] Von Balthasar, "Mary in the Church's Doctrine", p. 120.

Timothy: "For there is one God, and there is one mediator between God and men, the man Christ Jesus, who gave himself as a ransom for all" (1 Tim 2:5–6).

This unique mediation of Christ does not exclude mediation in a subordinate way by the saints. It is normal in the Church that we ask the martyrs and other saints to pray for us. We even ask priests and, indeed, fellow Christians, to pray for us. Even more, then, can we ask the Blessed Virgin Mary to intercede for us. The role of the Virgin of Nazareth as Mother of all believers in no way obscures or diminishes the unique mediation of Christ. Indeed, it rather shows its power. Mary mediates in Christ and subordinately through Christ. The Second Vatican Council is clear: "All the salvific influence of the Blessed Virgin on men originates, not from some inner necessity, but from the divine pleasure. It flows forth from the superabundance of the merits of Christ, rests on His mediation, depends entirely on it and draws all its power from it. In no way does it impede, but rather does it foster the immediate union of the faithful with Christ" (*LG* 60). "The Church does not hesitate to profess this subordinate role of Mary. It knows it through unfailing experience of it and commends it to the hearts of the faithful, so that encouraged by this maternal help they may the more intimately adhere to the Mediator and Redeemer" (*LG* 62).

Since Mary is our Mother in the order of grace, she takes care of us as a mother. By accepting to be the Mother of the Redeemer, she became associate or cooperator in the mission of the Redeemer, especially through her actions and sufferings. Since she herself was made full of grace, she was prepared by Divine Providence for this subordinate mediation. "With the redeeming death of her Son," says Saint John Paul II, "the maternal mediation of the handmaid of the Lord took on a universal dimension, for the work of redemption embraces the whole of humanity. Thus there is manifested in a singular way the efficacy of the one and universal mediation of Christ 'between God and men'. Mary's cooperation shares, in its subordinate character, in the universality of the mediation of the Redeemer, the one Mediator" (*RM* 40).

This consideration of the role of Mary as Mediatrix, under Christ, is a great encouragement to Marian devotion.

To Jesus through Mary is therefore not an empty slogan but, rather, a summary statement of true devotion to the Blessed Virgin Mary that leads us to Christ, the one Redeemer and Mediator. The Second Vatican Council charges that "practices and exercises of piety, recommended by the magisterium of the Church toward her in the course of centuries, be made of great moment, and those decrees, which have been given in the early days regarding the cult of images of Christ, the Blessed Virgin and the saints, be religiously observed" (*LG* 67). The council urges theologians and preachers that in treating of the unique dignity of the Mother of God, they avoid both the falsity of erroneous exaggeration and the excess of narrow-mindedness. They are to present the authentic image of the Virgin as it is given us in Holy Scripture, tradition, the sacred liturgy, and the holy Fathers and approved Doctors of the Church.

~

6

The Sacred Liturgy
and Marian Devotion

The sacred liturgy is the public worship of the Church. It is worship that Christ, as our Priest and Head of the Church, offers to his Eternal Father. In the liturgy, Christ associates the Church, his Bride, with himself in the offering of worship. That is why the Second Vatican Council says that "in the liturgy the whole public worship is performed by the Mystical Body of Jesus Christ, that is, by the Head and His members."[1]

Since the Blessed Virgin Mary is the Mother of the Redeemer, the most distinguished member of the Church, and indeed the Mother of the Church, and since she was the associate of the Redeemer in the mysteries of Christ, the sacred liturgy has given her an honored place. Indeed "both in the East and in the West the highest and purest expressions of devotion to the Blessed Virgin have sprung

[1] Second Vatican Council, Constitution on the Sacred Liturgy *Sacrosanctum Concilium*, December 4, 1963, no. 7 (hereafter cited as *SC*).

from the liturgy or have been incorporated into it"
(*MC* 15). Most prominent is the commemoration of
our Blessed Lady in the Eucharistic Prayer in every
Mass. In view of the fact that the Eucharistic Sacrifice is the supreme act of Christian worship, "this
daily commemoration, by reason of its place at the
heart of the divine Sacrifice, should be considered
a particularly expressive form of the veneration that
the Church pays to the 'Blessed of the Most High'
(cf. Lk. 1:28)" (*MC* 10). As we proceed in these
reflections, it will become clearer how the Roman
liturgy as a whole is a splendid illustration of the
Church's devotion to the Blessed Virgin.

The Advent liturgy is one of the earliest evidences
of the veneration given to the Mother of God by
the Church. Devotion to Mary is thus not separated from its necessary point of reference, which
is Christ. Advent is a liturgical period particularly
suited to devotion to the Mother of the Lord. The
great Solemnity of the Immaculate Conception is
celebrated in the beginning of Advent on December 8. That whole season, together with the Christmas period, has Christ at the center, but also, at his
side, his Blessed Mother. "The Christmas season is
a prolonged commemoration of the divine, virginal
and salvific motherhood of her whose 'inviolate virginity brought the Savior into the world'" (*MC* 5).

Christmas is followed by the Feast of the Holy Family and then by the Solemnity of Mary, the Holy Mother of God. The place of Mary in all these celebrations is clear. So is her role in the Solemnity of the Epiphany and in the Feast of the Presentation of the Child Jesus in the temple.

The rest of the liturgical year is punctuated with celebrations in honor of the Mother of God. The Annunciation on March 25 indicates the great event of the heavenly messenger coming to the Virgin of Nazareth to announce the greatest news of the Incarnation of the Word. The Visitation is celebrated on May 31, the Assumption on August 15, the Queenship of Mary on August 22, her Nativity on September 8, and her Sorrows on September 15.

Other Marian liturgical celebrations that can be mentioned here refer to shrines, places, or aspects of her life. Examples are Our Lady of Lourdes on February 11, Our Lady of Fatima on May 13, the memorial of her Immaculate Heart on the day after the Solemnity of the Sacred Heart of Jesus, Our Lady of Mount Carmel on July 16, Our Lady of the Rosary on October 7, the Presentation of Our Lady on November 21, and Our Lady of Guadalupe on December 12. There are, moreover, many Marian feasts or memorials approved for local churches or for religious congregations. And there are the Saturdays in Ordinary Time when there are no obligatory memorials. All this goes to show that veneration for the Blessed Mother of God accompanies the Church throughout the liturgical year.

The sacred liturgy highlights Mary's intercessory role. The public worship of the Church appreciates the importance of intercessory prayer. In the liturgy, the Church prays in general for herself, for the world, for the just, for sinners, for justice and peace, and for the living and the dead. The Church is aware of how Moses interceded for the people of Israel and averted God's punishment that would have fallen upon them, as the psalmist says: "He said he would destroy them —had not Moses, his chosen one, stood in the breach before him, to turn away his wrath from destroying them" (Ps 106:23).

Jesus Christ is our great intercessor. But the Church also has recourse to the Blessed Virgin Mary and the saints for intercession. In the Solemnity of All Saints, the Church asks to be heard by God through "the abundance of intercessors". The Church cannot forget the power of intercession that Mary exercised at the wedding feast of Cana.

Making allowance for the brevity characteristic of the Roman liturgy, it is really impressive to go through the Roman Missal and note the references

to Mary's intercession in celebrations in honor of
Our Blessed Mother. For example, on the Solemnity
of the Immaculate Conception, the Church in the
Collect prays God to grant that, as he preserved the
Blessed Virgin Mary from every stain, "so, through
her intercession, we, too, may be cleansed and ad-
mitted to your presence." In the Prayer over the Offerings on the Feast of the Holy Family, the Church
prays: "We offer you, Lord, the sacrifice of concili-
ation, humbly asking that, through the intercession
of the Virgin Mother of God and Saint Joseph, you
may establish our families firmly in your grace and
your peace." Similar references to the intercession
of Our Lady are to be found in the Collects of the
Solemnity of Mary, the Holy Mother of God, of the
Friday of the Fifth Week of Lent, of the memorial
of Our Lady of Lourdes, of the memorial of the Immaculate Heart of Mary, and of most of the other
Marian celebrations. The Collect of the memorial
of Our Lady of Mount Carmel is worth quoting in
full: "May the venerable intercession of the glorious
Virgin Mary come to our aid, we pray, O Lord, so
that fortified by her protection, we may reach the
mountain which is Christ."

In the Collect of the memorial of Our Lady of
Guadalupe, on December 12, the Church shows
beautiful trust in her power of protection: "O God,
Father of mercies, who placed your people under

the singular protection of your Son's most holy
Mother, grant that all who invoke the Blessed Virgin
of Guadalupe, may seek with ever more lively faith
the progress of peoples in the ways of justice and of
peace." The Prayer over the Offerings on the Solemnity of the Assumption has special warmth about it:
"May this oblation, our tribute of homage, rise up
to you, O Lord, and through the intercession of the
most Blessed Virgin Mary, whom you assumed into
heaven, may our hearts, aflame with the fire of love,
constantly long for you."

Considering that the "liturgy is a constitutive element of the holy and living Tradition", that is, that
the "law of prayer is the law of faith" (*lex orandi, lex
credendi*, or *legem credendi lex statuat supplicandi*, according to Prosper of Aquitaine; see *CCC* 1124), liturgical formulae do show our faith. The Church believes
as she prays. From the above and similar liturgical expressions of belief in the intercessory power of the
Blessed Virgin Mary, the Church is teaching us how
to pray. Marian devotion has strong foundations in
our faith.

There are other liturgical texts that show the faith of the
Church in the Mother of God and therefore teach
us how to pray.

The Lectionary has many rich biblical readings for
celebrations in honor of the Blessed Virgin Mary.

The *Liturgy of the Hours,* sometimes called the *Divine Office* or the *Breviary,* has many hymns, texts, prayers of the faithful, and beautiful concluding Marian hymns and antiphons after Compline or Night Prayer.

In the baptismal rite, at religious profession and at the consecration of virgins, and in prayers for the dying, for the dead, and for those who mourn, there are references to the intercessory role of the Blessed Virgin Mary.

In summary, this brief review of the place that the sacred liturgy gives to veneration of our Blessed Mother shows that the Roman liturgy, as renewed under the pontificate of Blessed Paul VI, properly considers the Blessed Virgin in the mystery of Christ and recognizes her singular place in Christian worship. As Mother of God and associate of the Redeemer, she is rightly honored by the tradition of the Church and by the liturgical movement preceding the Second Vatican Council. Christians who venerate Our Lady today have very strong liturgical reasons for this devoted attitude. Marian piety leads us to a greater participation in the mysteries of Christ and helps to assure that sound faith sufficiently supports affectivity in our respect for the Blessed Mother.

～

7

Mary's Faith

The followers of Christ who are devoted to the Blessed Virgin Mary admire her because of her many virtues, such as her love of God and neighbor, her obedience to the divine will, her trust and hope in God, her humility, her virginity, her dedication to the mission of the Redeemer, and her unfailing faith. This chapter will focus on the faith of Mary.

Faith is of fundamental importance in our relations with God. By faith we accept what God has said or promised; we trust in him and entrust ourselves to him; and we live our lives in line with that trust. "Faith", says the Letter to the Hebrews, "is the assurance of things hoped for, the conviction of things not seen" (Heb 11:1). Faith is both a theological virtue given by God as grace and an obligation that flows from the first commandment of God. Faith is a gift of God, a supernatural virtue infused by him. It is not arrived at as a result of logic or human reasoning, although theology can prove that it is reasonable to believe God. "To make this act of faith, the grace of

God and the interior help of the Holy Spirit must precede and assist, moving the heart and turning it to God, opening the eyes of the mind and giving 'joy and ease to everyone in assenting to the truth and believing it.' "[1] When God speaks, man should listen and accept. " 'The obedience of faith' (Rom. 16:26; see 1:5; 2 Cor 10:5–6) 'is to be given to God who reveals, an obedience by which man commits his whole self freely to God' " (DV 5).

The Blessed Virgin Mary showed her faith on many occasions. When the Archangel Gabriel came to her in Nazareth and announced that she would conceive and bear a Son while remaining a virgin, Mary believed, although such a wonder had not taken place anywhere before that day. When the same archangel told her that her kinswoman Elizabeth was with child, Mary believed and went with haste to visit her and be of help. When it was time for her to give birth to the Son of God in Bethlehem, and she and Joseph found no suitable place and had to settle for a manger, Mary did not begin to doubt whether the Child was really the Son of the Most High, as she had been told at the Annunciation (Lk 1:35). When the angel came to Joseph and ordered him to take

[1] Second Vatican Council, Dogmatic Constitution on Divine Revelation *Dei Verbum*, November 18, 1965, no. 5 (hereafter cited as *DV*); see also DH 377, 3010; and *CCC* 153.

the Child and the mother and go to Egypt, Mary did not doubt nor did she insist that such a burdensome message had to be given to her in person.

During the years of the hidden life of Jesus in Nazareth, Mary continued to believe in her Son. "Every day Mary is in constant contact with the ineffable mystery of God made man, a mystery that surpasses everything revealed in the Old Covenant. . . . Living side by side with her Son under the same roof, and faithfully persevering 'in her union with her Son,' she 'advanced in her pilgrimage of faith' " (*RM* 17). When Jesus at the age of twelve was found on the third day in the Jerusalem temple by Mary and Joseph and he gave them a reply that they did not understand, Mary continued to believe in him as the Son of God. At the wedding feast of Cana, Mary's appeal to Jesus in a few words for a miracle and her advice to the servants after an apparent refusal by her Son were manifestations of her deep faith in her Son as Son of God. On Calvary, Mary was present as Jesus underwent untold suffering and humiliation. The sword of martyrdom pierced her motherly heart, and she continued to believe in her Son as the anointed of the Most High. She certainly believed that he would rise again, and she lived Holy Saturday in that faith, so that she can in a sense be called the woman of faith on Saturday. It is no wonder that in the Roman Rite, Saturdays in Ordinary

Time when there is no obligatory memorial are dedicated to her. United in prayer with the Apostles after the Ascension of Christ, she was a pillar of faith for the early Church, which awaited the coming of the Holy Spirit.

Mary's faith has been compared to the faith shown by Abraham, whom Saint Paul calls "our father in faith" (see Rom 4:12). Abraham "in hope . . . believed against hope, that he should become the father of many nations" (Rom 4:18). Mary, at the Annunciation, having professed her virginity, believed that through the power of the Holy Spirit she would become the Mother of God's Son as the angel had revealed. Therefore, Saint John Paul II could say that "in the salvific economy of God's revelation, Abraham's faith constitutes the beginning of the Old Covenant; Mary's faith at the Annunciation inaugurates the New Covenant" (*RM* 14). In the living of this faith, Mary grew in her "pilgrimage of faith" (*LG* 58) and in her "obedience of faith" right up to the supreme moment of Calvary. While on Mount Moriah, God spared Abraham the final sacrifice of his son Isaac because Abraham had shown such great faith; on Mount Calvary, no angel intervenes, and the Son of Mary is sacrificed in his Mother's very presence.

Mary's faith is praised. Elizabeth was the first to do so: "Blessed is she who believed that there would be a fulfilment of what was spoken to her from the Lord" (Lk 1:45). Mary was being praised by Jesus, without a mention of her name, when Our Savior declared blessed those who hear the word of God and keep it (see Lk 11:28). Mary was the first of those who so believe and act. Moreover, when Jesus replied: "'Who are my mother and my brethren?' And looking around on those who sat about him, he said, 'Here are my mother and my brethren! Whoever does the will of God is my brother, and sister, and mother'" (Mk 3:33–35), this might appear to be a rebuff to his Mother. But it was not, because Mary, more than any of the Apostles, is the first of those who do the will of God.

Saint Augustine praises Mary's faith and says that when the angel spoke to her she was so full of faith that she conceived the Word of God in her mind before conceiving him in her womb.

The Church is in admiration of Mary's example and prays thus in the Collect of the Mass for December 20: "O God, eternal majesty, whose ineffable Word the immaculate Virgin received through the message of an Angel and so became the dwelling-place of divinity, filled with the light of the Holy Spirit; grant, we pray, that by her example we may in humility hold fast to your will."

Mary's total Yes to God is for us a shining example. When the Archangel Gabriel brought her what has to be regarded as God's proposal to her, he waited for her acceptance. The Virgin's response was one of total submission, without conditions. It was a Yes spoken by the whole person, spirit and body, without any restrictions. Mary offered her entire human nature as a locus for the Incarnation of the Word. And the Word was made flesh and dwelt among us. And we can note that the Virgin Mary, in her total trust in Divine Providence, left it to God to determine how Joseph was to be informed about the unique mystery that was taking place.

Our devotion to Mary must include our striving to say an unconditional Yes to God in both the small and the bigger details concerning our earthly pilgrimage. It is true that in the case of Mary, her Immaculate Conception, or total freedom from original sin, joined with her fullness of grace as declared by the archangel, made it in a way less difficult for her than it is for us to say a total Yes to God. Nevertheless, we have to keep up the struggle, even with our wounded human nature, to learn from our Blessed Lady to let God's will be our guide.

The dark night of faith comes to most of us sometime if we live long enough. There come times when our faith is really tested. Events that we do not understand may take place in our lives. Delights that one used to have in prayer may become rare or seem to disappear. Trials of various kinds begin to shake our faith. We seem to be in the dark. We do not see clearly the hand of God in events taking place.

At such times, we need to have recourse to Mary. She also passed through the dark night of faith. Every detail in the mystery of Christ was not made clear to her from the beginning of her Yes to God's salvific plan. For example, when she and Joseph found the Child Jesus in the temple after a three-day agonizing search for him, his response to his Mother's quiet statement of sorrow was: "How is it that you sought me? Did you not know that I must be in my Father's house?" The evangelist Luke then tells us that "they did not understand the saying which he spoke to them . . . and his mother kept all these things in her heart" (Lk 2:49–51). Saint Mark tells us that once when Jesus was preaching, his Mother and his brethren came, stayed outside, and expressed the desire to meet him. His response, after looking around at those who sat about him, was: "Here are my mother and my brethren! Whoever does the will of God is my brother, and sister, and mother" (Mk 3:34–35). And we are not told that he then received them. On their way back, his Blessed Mother must have been reflecting on the event. It was a dark night of faith for her. On Calvary, the test of her faith reached its height. The archangel's promise of a Messiah Son of the Most High who would be given the throne of his father David, who would reign over the house of Jacob forever, and whose kingdom would have no end (see Lk 1:32–33), all seemed to be eclipsed. It is also to be noticed that Jesus addressed her as "Woman" both at the significant event of his miracle at the wedding feast at Cana (see Jn 2:4) and at the supreme moment of his telling her from the Cross to take John as her son (see Jn 19:26). Did Mary at the time understand all the implications of Christ's use of this solemn term to refer to her? We do not know. Did Mary keep these "words", pondering them in her heart? We do not know. But what we do know is that the Blessed Virgin emerged admirably in her pilgrimage of faith all through the dark night. She is our model.

The faith of Mary was great and deep. We need to fly to her patronage and beg her to obtain for us something of her total Yes to God. The Second Vatican Council wants true Marian veneration to show itself in good works and true faith: "Let the faithful remember moreover that true devotion consists neither in sterile or transitory affection, nor in a certain vain credulity, but proceeds from true faith, by which we are led to know the excellence of the Mother of God, and we are moved to a filial love toward our mother and to the imitation of her virtues" (LG 67).

Mary's Assumption into heaven is like a crowning of her faith, her total Yes to God, her total availability to God in the history of salvation. As the Servant of God Pope Pius XII defined this dogma on November 1, 1950, "the Immaculate Mother of God, the ever Virgin Mary, having completed the course of her earthly life, was assumed body and soul into heavenly glory."[2] Mary is the first creature to benefit from the graces of the Resurrection of Jesus. As the pope explains in the document just quoted,

God, who from all eternity regards Mary with a most favorable and unique affection, has "when the fullness of time came" put the plan of his providence into effect in such a way that all the privileges and prerogatives he had granted to her in his sovereign generosity were to shine forth in her in a kind of perfect harmony. . . . She, by an entirely unique privilege, completely overcame sin by her Immaculate Conception, and as a result she was not subject to the law of remaining in the corruption of the grave, and she did not have to wait until the end of time for the redemption of her body.[3]

The pope in paragraph 21 quotes Saint John Damascene:

It was fitting that she, who had kept her virginity intact in childbirth, should keep her own body free from all corruption even after death. It was fitting that she, who had carried the Creator as a child

[2] Pius XII, Apostolic Constitution Defining the Dogma of the Assumption *Munificentissimus Deus*, November 1, 1950, no. 44, in DH 3903.

[3] Ibid., 3, 5.

at her breast, should dwell in the divine taberna-
cles. It was fitting that the spouse, whom the Father had taken to himself, should live in the divine
mansions. It was fitting that she, who had seen her
Son upon the cross and who had thereby received
into her heart the sword of sorrow which she had
escaped in the act of giving birth to him, should
look upon him as he sits with the Father. It was
fitting that God's Mother should possess what belongs to her Son, and that she should be honored
by every creature as the Mother and as the handmaid of God.[4]

Mary's strong faith and her great privilege of the
Assumption encourage us to say a total Yes to God
in all the details of our daily life, while we travel as
pilgrims on earth toward our heavenly homeland.

∼

---

[4] Saint John Damascene, *Encomium in Dormitionem Dei Gene-
tricis semperque Virginis Mariae*, hom. II, 14; also in *Liturgy of the
Hours*, August 15, second reading of the Office of Readings.

8

Examples of Some Saints

While visiting her kinswoman Elizabeth, the Blessed
Virgin Mary had prophesied: "Henceforth all generations will call me blessed" (Lk 1:48). And so it has
been. Saint after saint in the history of the Church
has called Mary blessed. Their devotion to her has
been manifested in doctrine, homilies, hymns, mu-
sic, and art. Some of them have defended the true
teaching of the faith against the errors of heretics and
have contributed to the formulation of doctrine in
such ecumenical councils as those of Ephesus and
Constantinople. They have lived lives of sustained
effort to imitate her virtues and to share their veneration of her greatness with other followers of Christ.
Here we shall select only a few examples of the many
saints who have shown special Marian devotion.

Among the early Greek and other Oriental saints, the following are outstanding for their Marian doctrine
and devotion. Saint Cyril of Alexandria contributed
much to the Council of Ephesus (in the year 431),
which defined the dogma of Mary, Mother of God
(*Theotokos*). Saint Ephrem the Syrian was a poetic

genius and was called "the lyre of the Holy Spirit". He tirelessly sang of the Mother of God and left a mark on the whole tradition of the Syriac Church. Saint Gregory of Narek, an outstanding glory of the Church in Armenia, with powerful poetic inspiration pondered on the different aspects of the mystery of the Incarnation and in each of them sang and extolled the extraordinary dignity and magnificent beauty of the Virgin Mary, Mother of the Word made flesh.

In the Byzantine liturgy, the Anaphora, or Eucharistic Prayer, of Saint John Chrysostom is famous. In it, after the epiclesis, the community sings in honor of Our Blessed Mother: "It is truly just to proclaim you blessed, O Mother of God, who are most blessed, all pure and Mother of our God. We magnify you who are more honorable than the Cherubim and incomparably more glorious than the Seraphim. You who, without losing your virginity, gave birth to the Word of God. You who are truly the Mother of God" (quoted in *RM* 32).

Very devoted to Our Lady were also Saints John of Damascus, Proclus of Constantinople, Germanus of Constantinople, Modestus of Jerusalem, Andrew of Crete, and Sophronius, monk and patriarch of Jerusalem.

In the Latin Church, the leadership already given by Saint Ambrose and Saint Augustine in the praise of Mary was followed by many saints. Prominent among the saints who have sung the praises of Mary are Saints Anselm of Canterbury, Bernard of Clairvaux, who was an abbot, Albert the Great, Thomas Aquinas, Bonaventure, Gregory VII, Bernardine of Siena, Robert Bellarmine, Catherine of Siena, Francis of Sales, and Maximilian Maria Kolbe. In our times, the Servant of God Pope Pius XII and Pope Saint John Paul II have written admirably on the Virgin Mary. John Paul II was also famous for his pilgrimages to Marian sanctuaries and for the prayers he composed in her honor almost each time he went to pray at a new Marian shrine. Two other saints who wrote classics on the Blessed Mother now need special mention.

Saint Louis-Marie Grignion de Montfort is distinguished for his treatise *True Devotion to Mary*. "It was through the most holy Virgin Mary that Jesus came into the world," he wrote, "and it is also through her that he has to reign in the world. . . . Mary is the excellent masterpiece of the Most High, the knowledge and possession of which he has reserved to himself. Mary is the admirable Mother of the Son." The saint continues and says that Jesus calls her "by the name of 'woman' (Jn 2:4; 19:26), as if she were a stranger, although in his heart he esteemed and loved her above all angels and all men. Mary is the 'sealed fountain' (Cant 4:12), the faithful spouse of the Holy Ghost, to whom he alone has entrance.

Mary is the sanctuary and the repose of the Holy Trinity, where God dwells more magnificently and more divinely than in any other place in the universe, not excepting his dwelling between the Cherubim and Seraphim."[1] Presenting and recommending the consecration of oneself to Jesus through Mary, Saint Louis-Marie writes: "The most perfect consecration to Jesus Christ is nothing else but a perfect and entire consecration of ourselves to the Blessed Virgin, and this is the devotion which I teach; or, in other words, a perfect renewal of the vows and promises of holy Baptism. This devotion consists, then, in giving ourselves entirely to Our Lady, in order to belong entirely to Jesus through her."[2] In the alternative Collect of the Mass for the memorial of this saint on April 28, the Church prays God that, following the same spiritual path, we may constantly spread God's kingdom.

Among those who have lived this true devotion to Mary as outlined by Saint Louis-Marie Grignion de Montfort, Pope Saint John Paul II is prominent. His episcopal and pontifical motto, *Totus Tuus* (entirely yours), reflects this devotion. Speaking of

---

[1] Saint Louis-Marie Grignion de Montfort, *True Devotion to Mary* (Rockford, Ill.: TAN, 1985) 1, 5.
[2] Ibid., 120–21.

Marian spirituality and its corresponding devotion, he writes: "In this regard, I would like to recall, among the many witnesses and teachers of this spirituality, the figure of Saint Louis-Marie Grignion de Montfort, who proposes consecration to Christ through the hands of Mary as an effective means for Christians to live faithfully their baptismal commitments. I am pleased to note that in our own time too new manifestations of this spirituality and devotion are not lacking" (*RM* 48).

Saint Alphonsus Maria de Liguori is for us a model of a Christian, a pastor, a bishop, and a theologian very devoted to Our Blessed Mother. In his classic *The Glories of Mary*, he writes that "lovers of this amiable Lady desire to praise her on all occasions, and to see her loved by the whole world, and never lose an opportunity, either in public or in private, of enkindling in the hearts of others those blessed flames of love with which they themselves burn towards their beloved Queen."[3] The saint praises Our Blessed Mother and recommends devotion to her:

As the glorious Virgin Mary has been raised to the dignity of Mother of the King of kings, it is not

[3] Saint Alphonsus Maria de Liguori, *Glories of Mary* (Brooklyn: Redemptorist Fathers, 1931), p. 30.

without reason that the Church honors her, and wishes her to be honored by all, with the glorious title of Queen. . . . Let us, then, have recourse, and always have recourse, to this most sweet Queen, if we would be certain of salvation; and if we are alarmed and disheartened at the sight of our sins, let us remember that it is in order to save the greatest and most abandoned sinners, who recommend themselves to her, that Mary is made the Queen of Mercy.[4]

Great saints have distinguished themselves by their devotion to the Immaculate Mother of God. They have blazed the way. We are not lacking examples to follow.

~

[4] Ibid., pp. 35, 43–44.

9

Marian Apparitions
and Shrines

Along the centuries and in different countries, there are reports that the Blessed Virgin Mary appeared to this or that person. There are also many churches or shrines built in honor of the Mother of God. Quite a number of them attract not a few pilgrims. In our reflection on Marian veneration, it is important to discuss what attitude a Christian should adopt toward the whole question of apparitions.

An apparition is in general an appearance to people on earth of a heavenly being, which could be Christ, Mary, an angel, or a saint. We can call it a supernatural vision. It can be a psychical experience, in which a person or object not accessible to normal human powers is seen and ordinarily also heard.

The apparitions of Jesus in his risen body to his disciples occurred between Easter and his Ascension into heaven. They are altogether exceptional and need to be treated apart from all other apparitions.

The risen Christ appeared to Mary Magdalen and other holy women, to Peter and the Twelve, to the two disciples on the road to Emmaus, and to five hundred of his disciples. Peter and the Twelve are the primary "witnesses to his resurrection" (Acts 1:22). Some of the disciples, like the Apostle Thomas, did not at first believe that the vision of Christ was real and that Christ had risen from the dead. They had not yet recovered from the shock of the Passion and death of their Master. The risen Christ strengthened their faith. It is not correct to imagine that the Resurrection of Christ was produced by the faith (or credulity) of the Apostles. "On the contrary their faith in the Resurrection was born, under the action of divine grace, from their direct experience of the reality of the risen Jesus" (*CCC* 644).

Some apparitions are recorded in Holy Scripture, such as those of God to Abraham (Gen 26:24), of an angel to Tobias (see Tob 3:16–17; 5:4–5), and of the Archangel Gabriel to Zechariah and to Mary (see Lk 1:11, 26). When a person claims to have received an apparition, the Church is rather slow and careful because illusions and hallucinations are common and the evil spirit can also intervene. The work of a spiritual director and sometimes of medical specialists can often be of help in the Church's investigation and evaluation. It is generally the diocesan bishop who has to undertake this discretionary work, while the authority of the pope or of his assistants in the Roman Curia would be involved only in rare cases.

If the message of a reported "apparition" is at variance with a revealed doctrine or the teaching of the Church, then this is a sign that it was not from heaven or that the "seer" has been misled. Even when Church authority pronounces positively on the authenticity of an apparition, such a decision is not regarded as infallible and is not imposed on the faithful for belief. Obviously, if Church authority has examined and pronounced against the authenticity of an "apparition", then the faithful should obey and have nothing to do with it.[1]

Messages or private revelations often follow from apparitions. The presumed seer can be convinced that he has received a message from heaven. Such messages are called private revelations to distinguish them clearly from revelation properly so called, which was concluded with the last of the twelve Apostles. Along the centuries, some private revelations have been recognized as authentic by the authority of the Church. "They do not belong, however, to the deposit of faith. It is not their role to improve or complete Christ's definitive Revelation, but to help live more fully by it in a certain period of history.

[1] See A. Buono, "Apparitions", in *Dictionary of Mary* (New York: Catholic Book Pub., 1997), pp. 46–50.

Guided by the magisterium of the Church, the *sensus fidelium* knows how to discern and welcome in these revelations whatever constitutes an authentic call of Christ or his saints to the Church" (*CCC* 67). When, therefore, the Church approves certain private revelations, such as that of the Blessed Virgin Mary to Saint Juan Diego in Mexico City or to Saint Bernadette Soubirous at Lourdes or to the three children in Fatima, they are to be accepted on the Church's judgment, but they do not form part of divine faith. Our Catholic faith is not based on apparitions and private revelations, although these can be very helpful in living the Gospel.

Reported Marian apparitions are many. Gottfried Hierzenberger and Otto Nedomansky document more than nine hundred reported Marian apparitions in the last two thousand years in their 560-page book, *Erscheinungen und Botschaften der Gottesmutter Maria* (Apparitions and messages of Mary Mother of God).[2]

Granted that the Church has approved only a few of these apparitions (whether at the level of the local Church or at the level of Rome), and granted that private revelations, even when approved by the

[2] Gottfried Hierzenberger and Otto Nedomansky, *Erscheinungen und Botschaften der Gottesmutter Maria* (Augsburg: Pattloch, 1993).

Church, are not imposed on the faithful as an object of Catholic faith, it still remains true that the Blessed Virgin Mary has *de facto* appeared and shown herself a mother in one century after another. She introduces no new revelation. She rather recalls us to focus attention on some aspect of the Gospel teaching. She is saying to us, as she did to the servants in Cana: "Do whatever he tells you" (Jn 2:5). The apparitions of the Blessed Virgin show her maternal love for her children. "She cares for the brethren of her Son, who still journey on earth" (*LG* 62). What our Blessed Mother tells us in many of the approved apparitions is to do penance, to abandon sin, to pray, to say the Rosary, to consecrate ourselves or our countries to her Immaculate Heart, and to frequent the Sacraments of Penance and the Holy Eucharist.

Pilgrims to Marian sanctuaries report conversions, a strengthening of faith, family reconciliations, brotherly love, physical healing, and the return to sacramental life. Marian shrines are filled with *ex voto* signs of gratitude for favors received.

Some approved Marian apparitions occurred in the following places: Guadalupe in 1531, Paris (to Saint Catherine Labouré) in 1830–1836, La Salette in 1846, Lourdes in 1858, Knock in 1879, Fatima in 1917, Beauraing in 1932, and Banneux in 1932.

Some Marian sanctuaries that attract pilgrims in the millions each year are Guadalupe, Aparecida, Lourdes, Fatima, Jasna Góra (or Czestochowa), Loreto, and Pompei.

Three early churches built in honor of Our Lady have special dignity and age. They are the Basilica of Saint Mary Major built in Rome after the Council of Ephesus, the Basilica of Santa Maria in Trastevere in Rome, and the Church of Saint Mary in Jerusalem.

Marian shrines, country by country, offer us an impressive list. Without suggesting that the following form anything near a complete list, here are some of the famous Marian shrines in many different countries:

> *Algeria*: Our Lady of Africa
>
> *Argentina*: Our Lady of Lujan
>
> *Austria*: Our Lady of Mariazell
>
> *Belgium*: Our Lady of Beauraing
>
> *Bolivia*: Our Lady of Copacabana
>
> *Brazil*: Our Lady Who Appeared (Aparecida)
>
> *Canada*: Saint Mary of the Hurons
>
> *Dominican Republic*: Our Lady of Altagracia
>
> *England*: Our Lady of Walsingham
>
> *France*: Our Lady of La Salette
>   Our Lady of Lourdes
>   Our Lady of the Miraculous Medal

Germany: Our Lady of Altötting
    Our Lady of Kevelaer

Greece: The Holy Mountain of Our Lady
    (Mount Athos)

India: Our Lady of Bandel
    Our Lady of Bandra

Ireland: Our Lady of Knock

Israel: Basilica of the Annunciation
    Basilica of the Nativity
    Church of the Dormition
    Church of the Visitation

Italy: Basilica of Saint Mary Major
    Holy House of Loreto
    Sanctuary of Pompei

Japan: Our Lady of Japan

Mexico: Our Lady of Guadalupe

Philippines: Our Lady of Safe Travel
    Our Lady of the Turumba

Poland: Our Lady of Czestochowa (Jasna Góra)

Portugal: Our Lady of Fatima

South Africa: Our Lady of Shongweni

Spain: Our Lady of Guadalupe of Estremadura
    Our Lady of Montserrat (Barcelona)
    Our Lady of the Pillar at Saragossa

Sri Lanka: Our Lady of Madhu

Switzerland: Our Lady of the Hermits

Uganda: Mary, Queen of Africa

USA: National Shrine of the Immaculate
   Conception

Vietnam: Our Lady of La Vang[3]

It is impressive that many countries have one or
more shrines in honor of the Mother of God. These
sanctuaries attract many pilgrims. Saint John Paul II
was famous for his visits to Marian shrines in his
104 papal travels outside Italy. Pope Francis visits
the Blessed Mother in the Basilica of Saint Mary
Major in Rome before and after each of his pastoral
visits outside Italy. Indeed, he went to this sanctuary the very day after his election as pope to entrust
his pontificate to the Blessed Virgin. These many
Marian shrines are a great encouragement to Marian
veneration.

∿

[3] See A. Buono, "National Shrines", in *Dictionary of Mary*,
pp. 448–54.

Marian Societies
and Associations

Devotion to the Blessed Virgin Mary throughout the centuries has given rise to the formation of various societies and associations in the Church. Many religious congregations have been founded in honor of the Mother of God. So have movements of various kinds, academic societies, confraternities, and schools of artists. Here are some examples of such Marian bodies.

Religious congregations honored with the name of Mary are quite numerous. The Marians of the Immaculate Conception are a religious congregation formed in 1673 by Saint Stanislaus Papczyński. They are also known as the Congregation of Marian Fathers of the Immaculate Conception. As a religious institute, they pledge support to the pope, spread devotion to the Blessed Virgin Mary as the Immaculate Conception, pray for the souls in purgatory, and undertake a variety of apostolic works. Although they are now an international organization, the Marians still have strong roots in Poland and place a great deal of emphasis on spreading the messages of Divine Mercy of Saint Faustina Kowalska.

The Company of Mary, also called the *Montfort Missionaries*, owes its origin to Saint Louis-Marie Grignion de Montfort. He began this religious institute in 1705 with just one missionary disciple, the aim being the preaching of missions and retreats under the standard and protection of the Blessed Virgin. The Company has grown to an international congregation of missionary priests and brothers serving in nearly thirty countries.

The Marianists, also called the Society of Mary, were founded in 1801 by Blessed William Joseph Chaminade. Marianist brothers and priests look to Mary as a model of faith and spirituality and are particularly engaged in educational work for the young.

The Marists were founded by Father Jean-Claude Colin in 1816. They have separate institutes for Brothers and for Sisters. They strive to imitate the Blessed Virgin in their spirituality and their daily work.

The Marist Brothers are a religious institute of Brothers founded in 1817 by Saint Marcellin Champagnat, a young French priest of the Marist Fathers. They are devoted to educational work throughout the world. Worthy of special mention is that in 2007 forty-seven Marist Brothers martyred in the Spanish civil war were beatified.

Among the many religious congregations for women in Nigeria that have Marian titles can be mentioned the Sisters of the Immaculate Heart of Mary, Mother of Christ, founded by Archbishop Charles Heerey, C.S.Sp., in 1937, and the Daughters of Mary Mother of Mercy, founded by Bishop Anthony Nwedo, C.S.Sp., in 1959. These sisters are engaged in educational work, medical service, works of social assistance, and parish services.

The high number of institutes of the consecrated life (that is, religious and members of secular institutes) that have Marian titles can be appreciated from the fact that the *Annuario Pontificio*, the yearbook of the Holy See, for the year 2015 lists no fewer than fifty-five institutes of men and 450 institutes of women with such titles.[1]

Movements of varying types have arisen in honor of the Blessed Virgin Mary. The Schoenstatt Movement was founded in Germany in 1914 by Father Joseph Kentenich as a means of promoting spiritual renewal in the Church. The movement emphasizes devotion to the Blessed Virgin as a model of love and purity. Many groups have been formed within the movement, including religious institutes.

The Militia of the Immaculata was founded in

[1] See *Annuario Pontificio, 2015* (Vatican City: Libreria Editrice Vaticana, 2015), pp. 1411–68; 1481–1681.

1917 by Saint Maximilian Maria Kolbe. Members are particularly devoted to the Immaculate Conception. They strive after spiritual renewal through the intercession of Mary Immaculate. Consecration to her and the wearing of the Miraculous Medal are dear to them.

The Legion of Mary was founded by Frank Duff in Dublin in 1921. Its spirituality is that of Saint Louis-Marie Grignion de Montfort as put forward in his book *True Devotion to Mary*. Members attend a weekly meeting, perform a weekly assignment of about two hours of apostolic work, and say a daily prescribed prayer. The preferred apostolate is home visitation. The Legion of Mary has spread to many countries as a powerful evangelizing organization and counts three million active members and around ten million auxiliary members.

The Blue Army of Our Lady of Fatima was founded in 1947 by Father Harold V. Colgan in New Jersey. It is focused on devotion to the Immaculate Heart of Mary, daily recitation of the Rosary, and diligent observance of the duties of one's state of life. This international organization was transformed into the World Apostolate of Fatima in 2005. Members today number more than twenty million.

Our Lady's Rosary Makers were formed as an organization in 1949 in Louisville, Kentucky, by Sylvan Mattingly, a Xaverian Brother. Inspired by the message of Our Lady of Fatima, he decided to form a Rosary-making club. The organization has grown and now has about seventeen thousand members who make and distribute around seven million cord and chain rosaries each year to those who request them in the mission countries.

The Focolare Movement, or the Work of Mary, was founded by Chiara Lubich in 1943 in Trent. This association of men and women includes people from various vocations in life. Its spirituality is concerned unity. Members strive to live the ideal, "That they may all be one" (Jn 17:21), for which Christ prayed. The movement has also distinguished itself in ecumenical contacts and in dialogue with people of other religions.

The Marian Movement of Priests was founded by Father Stefano Gobbi in 1972. It places special emphasis on the power of praying the Holy Rosary and on Eucharistic adoration as an effective means of strengthening the Church.

The Fatima Family Apostolate was founded in 1986 by Father Robert J. Fox in Hanceville, Alabama. Its mission is to promote the true message of Fatima and the sanctification of family life.

The Block Rosary Movement started in Nigeria in the 1960s as an association of children who gather in the evening to pray the Rosary together. No cleric was its founder, but priests and bishops have encouraged it. Its main activity is that of little children who gather in the evening in their quarter or "block" in the city; three children dress as Lucia, Jacinta, and Francisco, the three children who witnessed the 1917 apparitions at Fatima, and all make a procession along the city streets or village roads praying the Rosary. Sometimes catechetical instruction is added at the end. Many vocations to the sacred priesthood and to the religious life have arisen from the Block Rosary Movement.

Academic associations also honor the Mother of God. The Mariological Society of America was founded by Father Juniper B. Carol with the support of Father Charles Balic in 1949. It is a theological society dedicated to the study of the Virgin Mary along with an interest in encouraging Marian catechetics and Marian spirituality in the Americas. Members study and make known the role of the Blessed Virgin in the mystery of Christ and in the Church.

The Pontifical Academy of the Immaculate was founded in Rome in 1835 as a meeting point for young people for studies on and for piety toward the Blessed Mother. It began with students from the Roman Seminary and the Pontifical Gregorian University and soon received great scholars within its membership. The academy was made pontifical by Blessed Pope Pius IX in 1864. With the approval of Pope Pius XI in 1938, an annual offer of flowers to Mary Immaculate in the Piazza di Spagna on December 8 each year was added to its academic activity.

In 2012, the Pontifical Academy of the Immaculate was merged with the International Pontifical Marian Academy.[2]

The International Pontifical Marian Academy was founded by Father Charles Balic in 1946 with the aim of promoting scientific, speculative, and critico-historical studies on the Blessed Virgin Mary. The academy became an international center for the coordination of Marian studies by different Mariological societies around the world. From time to time, International Mariological-Marian Congresses are organized. In 1959, Pope Saint John XXIII gave it pontifical status. Since the year 1972 it has been administered by the Pontifical Antonianum University in Rome. Its president is one of the members of the Coordinating Council of Pontifical Academies in Rome.

Pious societies in honor of the Blessed Virgin Mary are numerous and take the form of confraternities, sodalities, scapular associations, and the like. People of the arts and the sciences, with or without formal associations, have given honor to the Mother of God by way of Marian icons, statues, pictures, poems, hymns, books, theatrical performances, and buildings. Communities love to dedicate church buildings to God with titles that refer to the Blessed Mother.

[2] Pope Benedict XVI, *Rescriptum ex Audientia*, December 4, 2012; *Acta Apostolicae Sedis* 105 (2013): no. 12, p. 1182.

For example, in Nigeria in 2016, thirteen out of fifty-four diocesan cathedrals have Marian titles.

Some media have Marian titles or promote devotion to our Blessed Mother. These media may be press, radio, or television initiatives or their derivatives.

The humble Virgin of Nazareth had prophesied during her visitation of Elizabeth: "Behold, henceforth all generations will call me blessed; for he who is mighty has done great things for me, and holy is his name" (Lk 1:48–49). Indeed, hundreds of institutes of the consecrated life, many Catholic movements, academic associations, devotional societies, and people of science and the arts have called Mary blessed. All those who venerate the Blessed Virgin Mary are greatly encouraged.

~

II

Marian Veneration in
Ecumenism and Evangelization

A devotee of the Blessed Virgin Mary is right to ask how Marian veneration enters into the ecumenical initiatives of individual Christians and also into the entire evangelizing activity of the Church.

Ecumenism refers to the whole spectrum of initiatives aimed at the reunion of Christians. Our Lord Jesus prayed that all his followers might be one, as he and the Eternal Father are one (see Jn 17:21). Through human fault, there have been divisions among Christians from the earliest centuries. The greatest division was that between the Church in the West and the Church in the East in 1054. In the West, the sad events of the rise of the Anglican and Protestant Churches and ecclesial communities in the sixteenth century are the most significant. "The attainment of union is the concern of the whole Church, faithful and shepherds alike", says the Second Vatican Council.[1] Since most of the readers of this book are

[1] Second Vatican Council, Decree on Ecumenism *Unitatis Redintegratio*, November 21, 1964, no. 5.

likely to be people who live in the so-called West,
reflections on ecumenism in the rest of this work
will have in mind contact with Churches and ecclesial communities that broke away from Rome in
the sixteenth century in that movement sometimes
called the Protestant Reformation.

Some Protestants when they meet Catholics express
doubts about Catholic Marian veneration. They ask
if Catholics have scriptural backing for this devotion.
They fear that devotion to Mary does not leave Jesus
central enough in Christian piety. Some of them go
farther and accuse Catholics of Mariolatry or of adoration of the Virgin Mary.

It is possible that such Protestants have met Catholics whose Marian devotion does not respect the
scriptural and dogmatic considerations that have earlier been set forth in this book. Some Catholics may
have contributed to making Mary less appreciated by
Protestants by honoring her in ways that are exag-
gerated and ill-advised and, above all, by not keep-
ing devotion to her clearly within a biblical frame-
work that shows her subordinate role with respect
to the Word of God, the Holy Spirit, and Jesus himself. But it is also possible that some Protestant objections or doubts arise out of anti-Catholic polemics or
from disguised rationalism regarding religious practice. There are also Protestants who wrongly think

that original and genuine Protestantism is opposed to veneration for the Blessed Virgin. Suggestions for a response may well begin from this last point.

Martin Luther, who is sometimes called "Father of the Reformation", accepted and asserted most of the Marian doctrines, such as the Divine Motherhood, the Immaculate Conception, and her perpetual virginity. He was not as clear about the invocation of Mary and the saints because he wanted to hold to Scripture alone, God alone, Christ alone, and grace alone (Luther doubted whether Scripture speaks of the invocation of Mary and the saints). Luther was, however, strong in proposing Mary and other saints as models for emulation. Unfortunately, later Lutherans and many other Protestants abandoned this basic element of Luther's faith with regard to the Blessed Virgin.[2]

Calvin was more silent on reverence for Mary, although he retained some Marian doctrines, such as her perpetual virginity. Zwingli was nearer to Luther in Marian doctrine. In England, the first reformers retained most Marian doctrines but criticized some liturgical or devotional manifestations.[3]

---

[2] See Peter Stravinskas, *Mary and the Fundamentalist Challenge* (Huntington, Ind.: Our Sunday Visitor, 1998), pp. 70–75.

[3] Ibid., pp. 75–79.

As this brief review reveals, not having a place for Mary in the Christian religion was not the intention of the earliest Protestant reformers, nor did they regard that stand as intrinsic to Protestantism. It is quite another matter that later Protestants often left Mary out of the picture. A careful approach should be maintained by Catholics who meet Protestants. In his third Advent sermon in the Vatican in December 2015, the Preacher of the Pontifical Household, Father Raniero Cantalamessa, gave an interesting account of the writings of a Lutheran woman, Mother Basilea Schlink. This Lutheran religious woman who founded a community of sisters in the Lutheran Church called the "Sisters of Mary", after recalling different texts by Luther on the Blessed Mother, wrote:

> Reading these words of Martin Luther, who revered the Mother Mary to the end of his life, observed the festivals of the Virgin Mary, and daily sang the Magnificat, we can sense how far the majority of us have drifted away from the proper attitude towards her. . . . Because rationalism accepted only that which could be explained rationally, church festivals in honor of Mary and everything else reminiscent of her were done away with in the Protestant Church. All biblical relationship to the mother Mary was lost, and we are still suffering from this heritage. When Martin Luther bids us to praise the mother Mary, declaring that she

can never be praised enough as the noblest lady and, after Christ, the fairest gem in Christendom, I must confess that for many years I was one of those who had not done so, although Scripture says that henceforth all generations would call Mary blessed (Luke 1:48). I had not taken my place among these generations.

Catholics who meet Protestants and discuss the Virgin Mary should bear this extraordinary testimony in mind.

In meeting Protestants, the following suggestions may be found useful. To be avoided are polemics and argumentation to see who will win. You can win an argument and lose a friend. The goodwill of the interlocutor should be presumed. Where this is obviously lacking, or where open aggressiveness is evident, it is doubtful if discussion is going to be very useful.

The Catholic should suggest quiet and prayerful reading of Holy Scripture, especially where references are made to our Blessed Mother, as indicated earlier in this book. It will be found that a meditative reading of the first two chapters of the Gospels according to Saint Matthew and Saint Luke and of the nineteenth chapter of Saint John will help to dispel many prejudices. Saint Paul tells the Romans that the Gospel "is the power of God for salvation to every one who has faith, to the Jew first and also to the Greek" (Rom 1:16).

The Catholic should also help the other Christian to realize that the early leaders of the Protestant Reformation appreciated the extraordinary graces that Divine Providence gave to Mary and that Martin Luther saw her as a model. Polemics that developed in history should not be allowed to block the respect that is due to the Blessed Virgin because of her role in the history of salvation. It is interesting to note that, at the invitation of the Catholic bishop of Tarbes and Lourdes, Bishop Jacques Perrier, the then Anglican archbishop of Canterbury, Dr. Rowan Williams, made a three-day visit to Lourdes in 2008 and, among other things, said: "Our prayer here must be that, renewed and surprised in this holy place, we may be given the overshadowing strength of the Spirit to carry Jesus wherever we go, in the hope that joy will leap from heart to heart in all our human encounters."[4]

Catholics should inform themselves well on what our faith teaches regarding the Virgin Mary, so that they can articulate it in a convincing way to other Christians. The Second Vatican Council urges Catholics to "assiduously keep away from whatever, ei-

[4] See Martin Beckford, in *The Telegraph*, September 24, 2008.

ther by word or deed, could lead separated brethren or any other into error regarding the true doctrine of the Church" (*LG* 67). Sound theological reflection on the mystery of the Incarnation, on the divine motherhood, on the Church, and on the role of the Virgin Mary as seen from Holy Scripture will not fail to show the firm foundations of Marian veneration.

Marian piety promotes evangelization. The Virgin Mary brought Jesus to the home of Zechariah and Elizabeth, and John the Baptist was sanctified even in his mother's womb. Mary presented the Child Jesus to the shepherds in Bethlehem and to the magi who came from the East. Mary stood at the foot of the Cross as associate of the Redeemer and accepted John as her spiritual son. She was, moreover, with the early Church between the Ascension and Pentecost, united in prayer. Mary's spiritual maternity "lasts until the eternal fulfilment of all the elect. Taken up to heaven she did not lay aside this salvific duty, but by her constant intercession continued to bring us the gifts of eternal salvation" (*LG* 62).

No doubt, the Holy Spirit is the principal agent of evangelization. As Blessed Paul VI explains: "It is He who impels each individual to proclaim the Gospel, and it is He who in the depths of consciences causes the word of salvation to be accepted and understood."[5] At the same time, the holy Mother of God is with the Church in the carrying out of the mandate to bring the Good News to all nations. This is visibly shown by the fact that "on the morning of Pentecost she watched over with her prayer the beginning of evangelization prompted by the Holy Spirit" (*EN* 82).

The Church is quite aware that in her evangelizing mission she very much stands in need of the motherly assistance of the Mother of the Redeemer. In the Collect of the Votive Mass of Our Lady, Mother of the Church, the Bride of Christ prays thus: "O God, Father of mercies, whose Only Begotten Son, as he hung upon the Cross, chose the Blessed Virgin Mary, his Mother, to be our Mother also, grant, we pray, that with her loving help your Church may be more fruitful day by day and, exulting in the holiness of her children, may draw to her embrace all the families of the peoples." A similar firm trust in the help of the Virgin Mary in the Church's evangelizing activity is manifested in the Prayer after Communion in that same votive Mass: "Having received the pledge of redemption and of life, we humbly pray, O

---

[5] Pope Paul VI, Apostolic Exhortation *Evangelii Nuntiandi*, December 8, 1975, no. 75 (hereafter cited as *EN*); see also Second Vatican Council, Decree on the Mission Activity of the Church *Ad Gentes*, December 7, 1965, no. 4.

Lord, that, with the Blessed Virgin's motherly help, your Church may teach all nations by proclaiming the Gospel and, through the grace of the outpouring of the Spirit, fill the whole earth.''

Both in the proposal of the Gospel of Jesus Christ to the followers of other religions who willingly receive this approach and in interreligious dialogue with some others, Marian devotion can be included. It is to be noted that the Qur'an has an honored place for the Blessed Virgin Mary and that quite a number of sincere Muslims respect Mary and are ready to discuss with Christians the Christian practice of Marian devotion. Christians who meet other believers should not fail to pray to the Holy Spirit for light and guidance on how best to proceed.

Convinced, therefore, of the role of the Mother of the Redeemer in the evangelizing mission of the Church, all Christians devoted to Mary should with confidence call on her as they seek to share the Good News of salvation in Christ with their brothers and sisters. The popes give us an example by their prayer to Mary before papal journeys and at all major Church events. All evangelizers—be they clerics, consecrated people, or the lay faithful—should fervently have recourse to Mary in all their initiatives at evangelization. Marian veneration is very positive in furthering evangelization.

12

Three Great Marian Prayers

We now need to reflect upon three great Marian prayers. They are biblically based; they are meditative; and they are suitable for all states and stages of the spiritual life. Devotees of Our Lady are familiar with them, but each person can make progress in the understanding of these prayers and in offering them daily. These prayers are the *Hail Mary*, the *Angelus*, and the *Holy Rosary*.

The Hail Mary has two parts. It begins with the greeting from heaven pronounced by the Archangel Gabriel: "Hail Mary" (or Rejoice, Mary). It is God himself who sends his angel to greet the Virgin of Nazareth with these solemn words. We dare to take up this greeting with great respect.

"Full of grace, the Lord is with thee." Mary is full of grace because the Lord is with her. She is filled with the presence of him who is the source of all grace. "Rejoice and exult with all your heart, O daughter of Jerusalem! . . . The LORD, your God, is in your midst" (Zeph 3:14, 17). Mary is the ark of

the covenant, the place where the glory of the Lord
dwells. Mary, full of grace, is wholly given over to
him who has come to dwell in her and whom she is
about to give to the world.

"Blessed art thou among women and blessed is
the fruit of thy womb, Jesus." Elizabeth's greeting is
now our own. Elizabeth is the first of those who have
called Mary blessed. Mary is blessed among women
because she believed in what was told her by the
Lord. Abraham believed and became a blessing for
all the nations of the earth. Mary believed and became the Mother of believers. Through her all nations of the earth receive God's own blessing, the
Redeemer, Jesus, the "fruit of thy womb".

"Holy Mary, Mother of God". The Church opens
the second part of the *Hail Mary* by confessing Mary
to be the Mother of God. This Christological title
proclaimed by the Council of Ephesus is precious
to us. Mary's Son, Jesus, is the Second Person of the
Most Blessed Trinity who took on human nature.
We know that we can entrust all our cares and peti-
tions to her and, through her, abandon ourselves to
God's will.

"Pray for us sinners, now and at the hour of our
death." By begging Mary to pray for us, we acknowledge that we are poor sinners who need the help of
the Mother of Mercy now and at the critical moment of our death (see *CCC* 2676, 2677).

Devotees of Mary must never allow familiarity to make us forgetful of the biblical and Christian depth of the *Hail Mary*.

The Angelus is that prayer which in the Latin Church is said in the morning, at midday, and in the evening. It is biblical through and through. Its three short sentences are Christocentric: the message of the Incarnation, the Virgin's consent, and the realization of the Incarnation. One *Hail Mary* follows each of these three sentences, and thus we are given opportunity to linger with Our Blessed Mother in whom the Incarnation was realized.

The *Angelus* is simple in structure, biblical in character, historical in origin, because it is linked with prayer for peace and safety, and quasi-liturgical in its rhythm of morning, noon, and evening. It reminds us of the Paschal Mystery because it recalls the Incarnation and prays that we may be led through the Passion and Cross to the glory of the Resurrection. It is a prayer highly conducive to contemplation.

In our times, people worldwide are accustomed to the pope conducting the prayer of the *Angelus* at noon from his study window in the Vatican every Sunday. And people expect a brief "Angelus Message" from the Vicar of Christ afterward. It is usual for church bells to be rung in a special rhythm at the time of the *Angelus* and for Catholics to stop whatever else they are doing and offer this beautiful Marian invocation. It is impressive to see traders and clients stand in the Onitsha market in Nigeria, the biggest open market in West Africa, as soon as the bell rings, to say this prayer at midday. People who are not Catholics marvel at this open confession of faith. During Paschal time, the *Angelus* is replaced by the *Regina Coeli*, which is also deeply scriptural and Christological.

The Rosary is a longer Marian prayer that is also scriptural, Christocentric, and with deep roots in history. It is marked by the following elements: the Creed, the Our Father, and three Hail Marys, then one Our Father, ten Hail Marys, and one Glory be to the Father for each of the twenty decades. The three original sets of five decades each are the Joyful Mysteries, the Sorrowful Mysteries, and the Glorious Mysteries, to which were later added the Luminous Mysteries. The Rosary can be prayed in different ways: alone by oneself, in a group, in the family, in a Catholic community, or over the radio or television. It can be enriched with Bible readings, with short homilies, with hymns, or with moments of silence.

Traditionally promoted by the Order of Preachers (the Dominicans), the Rosary has been praised and recommended by many popes, such as Saint Pius V, Pius VI, Leo XIII, Pius XII, Saint John XXIII,

Blessed Paul VI, Saint John Paul II and Benedict XVI. Pope Pius XII in his letter to the archbishop of Manila in 1946 called the Rosary a "compendium of the entire Gospel". Saint John Paul II proclaimed a Year of the Rosary from October 2002 to October 2003. Saint Louis-Marie Grignion de Montfort, Saint Pio of Pietrelcina, and Blessed Bartolo Longo were very devoted to the Rosary.

The Rosary is a Gospel-inspired prayer. In it, reflection is focused on the principal salvific events accomplished in Christ, together with their effects on the Blessed Virgin Mary and on the infant Church. As can be seen, the concentration is Christocentric. This Christocentric emphasis of the Rosary is clearly evident, as was seen earlier: the first thirteen mysteries of the Rosary and all five Luminous Mysteries are about Jesus, and only the last two are explicitly about the Blessed Virgin Mary. "The Rosary is also *a path of proclamation and increasing knowledge*, in which the mystery of Christ is presented again and again at different levels of the Christian experience. Its form is that of a prayerful and contemplative presentation, capable of forming Christians according to the heart of Christ."[1] Those who pray the Rosary should not

---

[1] Pope John Paul II, Apostolic Letter on the Most Holy Rosary *Rosarium Virginis Mariae*, October 16, 2002, no. 17; emphasis added (hereafter cited as *RVM*).

stay at the level of repetitive prayer. This Marian prayer is highly conducive to contemplation with its quiet rhythm and lingering pace dotted with the sacred names of Jesus and Mary and with the doxology, *Gloria Patri*. "The Rosary", says Saint John Paul II, "belongs among the finest and most praiseworthy traditions of Christian contemplation. Developed in the West, it is a typically meditative prayer, corresponding in some way to the 'prayer of the heart' or 'Jesus prayer' which took root in the soil of the Christian East. . . . [It] has the simplicity of a popular devotion but also the theological depth of a prayer suited to those who feel the need for deeper contemplation" (*RVM* 5, 39).

The Second Vatican Council in no way discouraged the praying of the Rosary. Of course the council stressed that "every liturgical celebration, because it is an action of Christ the priest and His Body which is the Church, is a sacred action surpassing all others; no other action of the Church can equal its efficacy by the same title and to the same degree" (*SC* 7). But the council also declared in the same document that "the sacred liturgy does not exhaust the entire activity of the Church" (*SC* 9). There is room, too, for penance, catechetics, sacred reading, and popular devotion. Indeed "not only does this prayer [the Rosary] not conflict with the Liturgy, *it sustains it*, since it serves as an excellent introduction and a faithful echo of the Liturgy, enabling people to participate fully and interiorly in it and to reap its fruits in their daily lives" (*RVM* 4). Blessed Paul VI had earlier given the same testimony: "The Rosary is an exercise of piety that draws its motivating force from the liturgy and leads naturally back to it, if practiced in conformity with its original inspiration" (*MC* 48).

Saint Louis-Marie Grignion de Montfort calls the Rosary "a priceless treasure which is inspired by God . . . a divine summary of the mysteries of the life, passion, death and glory of Jesus and Mary."[2] Devotees of our Blessed Mother will find this book of Saint Louis-Marie precious and most helpful.

These considerations are a great encouragement to all followers of Christ to pray the Holy Rosary with devotion every day.

∿

---

[2] Saint Louis-Marie Grignion de Montfort, *The Secret of the Rosary* (New York, 2002), pp. 9, 10.

13

Forward with
Marian Veneration

In this concluding chapter, a summary is offered in five considerations to promote a healthy and robust devotion to the Most Blessed Virgin Mary.

One must first be clear on the foundational dogma that Jesus Christ is our one and only way to the Father. Jesus is the way, the truth, and the life. No one comes to the Eternal Father except through him (see Jn 14:6). Jesus is our ultimate model and exemplar. Him we must follow and seek to imitate. Marian devotion helps us to do this, to live as authentic Christians, to be renewed in Christ, and thus to see produced in ourselves characteristics of Christ, the only begotten Son of the Father and Son of the Virgin Mary.

Bishops and priests who guide the people of God should do all that is possible to orient properly the people's Marian devotion. "It is supremely fitting", says Blessed Paul VI, "that exercises of piety directed towards the Virgin Mary should clearly express the Trinitarian and Christological note that is intrinsic and essential to them" (*MC* 25). Mary is daughter of the Father, Mother of the Son, and temple or mystical bride of the Holy Spirit. For her role as associate of the Redeemer, the Eternal Father from all eternity chose her, and the Holy Spirit endowed her with extraordinary graces and overshadowed her. Marian veneration should always lead to Christ the Savior and, through him, to the Father in the unity of the Holy Spirit.

Due attention should be given to the role assigned by Divine Providence to the Blessed Virgin Mary in the working out of the history of salvation. This explains the importance of the sound biblical, dogmatic, and liturgical orientations that should be given to particular exercises of Marian piety. Many Catholics need help and encouragement in giving more place to the Bible in their Christian lives. The Second Vatican Council goes into some detail regarding the relationship between popular devotions and the sacred liturgy: "These devotions should be so drawn up that they harmonize with the liturgical seasons, accord with the sacred liturgy, are in some fashion derived from it, and lead the people to it, since, in fact, the liturgy by its very nature far surpasses any of them" (*SC* 13). Marian devotion is very conducive to this orientation.

Pastoral care is needed because errors of exaggeration can occur from time to time even in expressions of Marian devotion. The Second Vatican Council, says Blessed Paul VI, "authoritatively denounced both the exaggeration of content and form which even falsifies doctrine and likewise the small-mindedness which obscures the figure and mission of Mary" (*MC* 38). Devotional deviations, vain credulity that lacks serious commitment to living a good life and puts the emphasis on merely external practices, and also sterile and ephemeral sentimentality are very different from persevering and practical action. True devotion to Mary is vigorous and authentic. It leads its devotees to seek to imitate Mary in their lives, each person according to his vocation and mission. It does not dwell on a search for novelties and extraordinary phenomena. It avoids a one-sided presentation of the figure of Mary that stresses one element at the price of compromising the over-all picture of the Virgin given by the Gospel. "The ultimate purpose of devotion to the Blessed Virgin is to glorify God and to lead Christians to commit themselves to a life which is in absolute conformity with His will" (*MC* 39). "Blessed are those who hear the word of God and keep it!" (Lk 11:28). If the pastor keeps these criteria in mind, he will do well in directing Marian groups.

A word should be said about charismatic groups. In some places, there are Catholic charismatic groups

that privilege spontaneous personal prayer, prefer-
ably with biblical inspiration or overtones. This is
good and praiseworthy. However, it also happens
that some of these groups seem to discourage fixed
prayers like the Our Father, the Hail Mary, the
Rosary, and the *Memorare*. One approach is not opposed to the other. A spontaneous prayer based on
the Bible can also be inspired by our faith regarding the Blessed Virgin Mary. But it would not be
correct to ignore fixed prayers like the Our Father,
the Hail Mary, and the Rosary. Indeed, these prayers
are biblical and are hallowed by tradition. The Our
Father is given us by Christ himself. In favor of the
charismatic approach, one can say that it can encourage greater interiorization of religious sentiment and
of the expression of religious belief in prayer. This
legitimate tendency can and should be used to promote Marian devotion.

People who are sincerely and properly devoted
to the Virgin Mary should not be apologetic about
it. "The Church's devotion to the Blessed Virgin
is an intrinsic element of Christian worship" (*MC*
56). Marian devotion is firmly rooted in the revealed
word of God and has dogmatic foundations: Mary
is Mother of God, daughter of the Father, and temple of the Holy Spirit. Because of the extraordinary
graces she has received, Mary "far surpasses all crea-

tures, both in heaven and on earth" (*LG* 53). Mary is Mother and associate of the Redeemer, Mother of the Church, and intercessor for mankind before God. Mary's glory does honor to the whole of humanity, as Dante sings: "You have so ennobled human nature that its very Creator did not disdain to share in it. . . . Lady, thou art so great and so powerful, that whoever desires grace yet does not turn to thee, would have his desire fly without wings."[1] Mary is "our tainted nature's solitary boast", as the poet Wordsworth calls her and as earlier quoted.[2] "Hail, thou beauty of the human race", the Church salutes the Virgin Mary in the first verse of the Marian antiphon *Salve Mater Misericordiae*.

Go forward, therefore, without fear, devotees of the Blessed Virgin Mary, because Marian veneration has strong foundations. Together with the Church, joyfully and trustfully chant the antiphon:

> Loving Mother of the Redeemer,
> Gate of heaven, star of the sea,
> Assist your people who have fallen yet strive
>   to rise again.

[1] Dante, *La Divina Commedia, Paradiso* 33, 4–6; 13–15.
[2] William Wordsworth, "The Virgin", in *Ecclesiastical Sonnets*, part 2, 1822.

To the wonderment of nature you bore
  your Creator,
Yet remained a virgin after as before.
You who received Gabriel's joyful greeting,
Have pity on us poor sinners.

(Antiphon: *Alma Redemptoris Mater*)

Abbreviations

CCC: *Catechism of the Catholic Church.* 2nd ed. Vatican City: Libreria Editrice Vaticana; Washington, D.C.: United States Catholic Conference, 1997.

DH: Heinrich Denzinger. *Compendium of Creeds, Definitions, and Declarations on Matters of Faith and Morals.* Edited by Peter Hünermann; English edition edited by Robert Fastiggi and Anne Englund Nash. 43rd ed. San Francisco: Ignatius Press, 2012.

DV: Second Vatican Council. Dogmatic Constitution on Divine Revelation *Dei Verbum.* November 18, 1965.

EN: Pope Paul VI. Apostolic Exhortation *Evangelii Nuntiandi.* December 8, 1975.

LG: Second Vatican Council. Dogmatic Constitution on the Church *Lumen Gentium.* November 21, 1964.

MC: Pope Paul VI. Apostolic Exhortation for the Right Ordering and Development of Devotion to the Blessed Virgin Mary *Marialis Cultus.* February 2, 1974.

RM: Pope John Paul II. Encyclical Letter on the Blessed Virgin Mary in the Life of the Pilgrim Church *Redemptoris Mater*. March 25, 1987.

RVM: Pope John Paul II. Apostolic Letter on the Most Holy Rosary *Rosarium Virginis Mariae*. October 16, 2002.

SC: Second Vatican Council. Constitution on the Sacred Liturgy *Sacrosanctum Concilium*. December 4, 1963.

STh: Thomas Aquinas. *Summa Theologica*.